2

PERSPECTIVES ON AGING
AND HUMAN DEVELOPMENT Series

IN THE COUNTRY
OF THE OLD

EDITOR: JON HENDRICKS

Baywood Publishing Company, Inc.

Library of Congress Catalog Card Number: 79-65155
ISBN Number: 0-89503-015-2

Library of Congress Cataloging in Publication Data
Main entry under title:

In the country of the old.

(Perspectives on aging and human development series ; 2)
    Includes bibliographical references.
    1. Aged--Addresses, essays, lectures. 2. Old age--Social aspects--Addresses, essays, lectures.
3. Cross-cultural studies--Addresses, essays, lectures.
4. Social status--Addresses, essays, lectures.
5. Social role--Addresses, essays, lectures. I. Hendricks, Jon, 1943-   II. Series.
HQ1061.I48 1980   301.43'5   79-65155
ISBN 0-89503-015-2

preface

Aging represents a paradoxical chain of events. While individuals are often convinced their lives are like no one else's, gerontologists busy themselves making generalizations. On a personal level, there are innumerable events which serve to structure our personal situation to such an extent that it seems impossible that anyone could approximate what seems to be our unique situation. Despite this, those who study the aging process successfully apply the results of their investigations to describe or predict what happens over the lifecourse for most people. Clearly, there appears to be undeniable validity to either position. Aging is indeed an individual occurrence, structured by one's own biography. Yet our membership in a particular biological species and in identifiable social groupings insure certain parameters and constraints will delimit the arena within which personal choice will be exercised.

This volume, the second in the *Perspectives on Aging and Human Development* series, is designed to highlight the relationship between our broader cultural context and the role it plays in defining the shape of aging. Schooled as we are in the nuances of mainstream American aging patterns, it is sometimes difficult to realize that relativity is the name of the game. This is not to say that every cultural category will manifest homogeneous patterns unrelated to those characteristic of other groupings. It is only to suggest that ethnicity and culture are as important as age itself, sex, social class background or other such variables in determining subjective experience. Just as these articles have been selected to emphasize the differences which emerge from contextual factors, so too do they point out the many commonalities which cut across all manner of national or subcultural boundaries. In short, they provide a comparative measure of how individual aging is a reflection of the positions we occupy in our particular socio-cultural drama.

To set the stage, Part I presents two conceptual essays which will assist the reader in recognizing some dimensions of the relative patterns of aging. In their discussion of cultural considerations affecting the lives of us all, Maxwell and Silverman couch their thesis in terms of a shifting complex of role and status positions. Central to their considerations is the elderly's control of valued information; the greater the control, the greater the prestige. Accordingly, in those cultures undergoing rapid change, the information available from older members will tend to diminish with their participation in societal institutions following suit. The parallels between older people in industrializing cultures and

iii

those living in societies which have already undergone the change and are built on growth patterns requiring ever newer occupational skills will not be lost to the astute reader. In the second selection, Holmes furnishes as cogent an overview of the main themes of "anthropological gerontology" as exists in the literature. In referring to socio-cultural studies in this way, Holmes is not implying a disciplinary approach. The term simply refers to work which is comparative and focuses on the holistic nature of behavior and events. Having gained some appreciation of the types of factors likely to operate in a broad range of cultural contexts, the presentation can turn to a review of selected settings in order to assess the relative nature of the aging process.

Part II offers a brief look into the way aging is evaluated in a range of cultures. It is not intended as an exhaustive survey, only as an illustrative comparison of relativity which structures the life world. Press and McKool examine the prestige generating components of the social system insofar as the elderly are concerned. Basing their conclusions on their work in a number of peasant communities in Mexico and Guatemala, the authors contend that the forces of "modernization" turn out to be inimical to a positive evaluation of old people. In isolating four role-sets they feel are beneficial to the elderly, they also note the disadvantages accompanying the heterogeneity which goes hand in hand with increasing economic, industrial and social modernization. Shifting several thousand miles into the Pacific, Maxwell examines how contact with the industrial world has undermined the traditional status of aged Samoans. As marketing and exchange arrangements come to be modelled along Western lines, older people are deprived of their central importance in the affairs of everyday life and thereby forced to relinquish their authority and control. The same factors identified as disruptive in Meso-American cultures prove the same in Polynesian society.

Portugal is a country of contrasts. Her cities rank among the most modern in Europe while the rural areas are remarkably untouched by the commercialism and industrialism of the contemporary world. In his analysis of correlative status of old people residing in these areas, Lipman portrays the components upon which prestige and status are founded. He notes at least two dimensions must be taken into account in evaluating the position of the elderly, suggesting once again that it is not age *per se,* but domination over resources which determines the position occupied by the old people of a society. Shifting our attention somewhat, the next two selections look at differences within modern cultures. With so much at stake, it might reasonably be assumed that significant attitudinal differences between young and old will emerge in any culture where the basis of honorific prestige is changing. Though Sweden has long considered itself among the modern societies of the world, the transition has occurred within the lifetimes of some of its oldest members. It is not surprising that the old and young of Sweden may see things quite differently. Skoglund reports that indeed this is the case; distinct preferences do exist, though they are mediated by sex and social class variables. As a country with a stable population distribution and a high degree of industrialization, Sweden may well portend what lies ahead for cultures now undergoing the kinds of changes Sweden has already experienced. The final article in this section concentrates on the rural aged in Israel. As a modern culture, Israel is an anomaly, meeting the usual criterion of industrial cultures yet continuing to accord its elderly traditional deference. Berman surveys three rural environments and notes the extent to which changing economic conditions have begun to undermine the social standing of the elderly in a culture which has so far contradicted customary expectations.

Having seen the social meaning of aging in a number of cultures ranging along a "modernization" continuum, Part III turns attention to what it means to be a minority member and old in the United States. While we cannot assume a complete homogeneity within various subcultures, the experiences of the ethnic elderly must be evaluated in light of their cultural background. Yet this is also changing at a rapid pace; the immigrants of a generation ago, or the older members of ethnic groups of longer standing are not synonymous with their younger counterparts. Pierce, Clark and Kaufman look at ethnic identity across generations of Mexican and Japanese Americans. Wilson and colleagues compare Japanese and whites living in Hawaii. In both instances interesting cultural variations appear to affect the way people present themselves in their normal lives as well as their performance on specialized cognitive tests. Despite the cultural hegemony implicit in the two foregoing essays, isolated pockets of ethnicity continue to thrive even among Anglo-Americans. Lozier and Althouse report one such example found in Appalachia. Again it is evident that social standing within the community is based on earned credits and is an ever present aspect of adjustment and coping mechanisms. The remaining selection offers an illustrative look at Black aging. Jackson summarizes a number of social and health characteristics of aged Blacks and in her customary fashion calls for additional attention to exactly those areas in which Blacks have experienced the most difficulties.

table of contents

part one

THE ELDERLY IN CROSS-CULTURAL PERSPECTIVES: ROLE AND STATUS

chapter 1

INFORMATION AND ESTEEM: CULTURAL CONSIDERATIONS IN THE TREATMENT OF THE AGED[1]

Robert J. Maxwell, Ph.D. and Philip Silverman, Ph.D.

INTRODUCTION

ANTHROPOLOGISTS have not, on the whole, shown much interest in aging. With few exceptions, ethnographic reports seem to mention the aged only in passing, if at all, and then only in the context of quite general statements. The reader is left with the impression that the population being studied is made up of males in maturity, with women and children as peripheral figures. Even the culture and personality theorists, with their interest in the various stages of the life cycle, gave little attention to the aged. This neglect is odd, in view of the fact that, as Bromley (1966, p. 13) has pointed out, "we spend about one quarter of our lives growing up and three quarters growing old."

There are several reasons for this. Old age itself is not pleasant to contemplate: the biological changes associated with aging are those we ourselves will someday undergo. Moreover, the aged occupy the terminal stage of the life cycle, so that we know where they will be twenty years from now, whereas we don't know what will happen to the children in the community. In connection with this, old people are likely to be the guardians of the old traditions and not active agents of socio-cultural change, so they are of lesser theoretical interest. Finally, there are fewer old people around outside of relatively complex and industrialized societies.

Nevertheless, some descriptive material has appeared. Arensberg and Kimball (1940), Elwin's work on the Muria Gond (1947),

[1] Thanks are due to Susan Singer of Philadelphia; to the students in the cross-cultural methodology course given at The City College of New York (Spring, 1970), particularly Dorothy Burstyn and Mary McMecham; and to Pertti J. Pelto of the Department of Anthropology, University of Connecticut; all of whom lent their assistance to the preparation of this paper.

Spencer on Samburu "gerontocracy" (1965), Clark and Anderson (1967) on aged representatives of various ethnic groups in the San Francisco Bay Area, and some more abbreviated efforts (see Cowgill 1965; Maxwell 1970; Okada 1962a, 1962b; Rowe 1961; Shelton 1969) help to shed some light on the disposition of certain societies toward their older members.

Simmons' *The Role of the Aged in Primitive Society* (1945) deserves special mention as a more ambitious comparative work than the others. This volume, which stands as the first and only large-scale cross-cultural study of aging,[2] rich as it is in illustrative material, is unfortunately of limited value, largely because of its flawed methodology. In a sample of 71 societies, he includes several that are closely related—for example, the Polar Eskimo and the Labrador Eskimo; the Dieri and the Aranda of Australia. The problem with closely related societies, of course, is that, unlike closely related individuals, you don't know whether you are dealing with one case or two. In the absence of careful sampling procedures it is easy for generalizations drawn from the data to be awry. This alone would be enough to make Simmons' conclusions suspect, but, in addition, he had coded 240 culture traits in these 71 societies by himself, without providing explicit coding rules for the reader, so that the reliability of his data cannot be known. What, for example, is "phallicism" (p. 3)?

Finally, there are some errors in the statistical operations employed (see Correlation 1, Appendix A, p. 245) which cast doubt on his other procedures.

In the twenty-five years since the appearance of Simmons' book, the theory and methodology of comparative studies have come far and it is perhaps time to begin a reexamination of the problem of the aged in cross-cultural perspective.

It will be suggested here that information of varying utility is distributed throughout the sociocultural system. In industrialized societies characterized by artifactual storage of information and rapid sociocultural change, the information controlled by older people is rapidly rendered useless to society or—to the extent that

[2] Koty (1933) attempted to cover the ethnographic literature on the treatment of the aged and the sick before such data banks as the Human Relations Area Files made comparative research a more manageable task. Although his theoretical perspective is outdated, the book contains much useful information, particularly from Russian sources.

it is useful—is stored in books, archives, computers, or other artifacts. Both of these processes, rapid social change and artifactual storage, cause the participation of the aged in the social life of the community to decrease and become less important in terms of system maintenance and survival. This, in turn, causes respect for the aged to decline.

It is true that in some less complex and technologically simple societies the aged are killed or abandoned. The above proposition implies, however, that this may not necessarily involve a loss of respect for the aged. Under harsh environmental circumstances, where the group must move about periodically in search of food or water, it is absolutely necessary for group survival that the aged be sacrificed or abandoned if, in fact, they can not keep up with the rest of the group.

It will be hypothesized, then, the societies can be arrayed along a continuum, the basis of which is the amount of useful information controlled by the aged. This informational control will be reflected in the participation of the aged in community affairs, and their participation will, in turn, determine the degree of esteem in which they are held by the other members of the community. It is expected that this informational control, and consequently social participation, will decline with industrialization and rapid sociocultural change.

THEORY

One of the more fruitful models developed for the investigation of human societies has focused on information storage and exchange and may be described under the general rubric of systems theory.

Culture as a System

If a system is a bounded organization of dynamically related components, then any culture qualifies as a system by definition. A sociocultural system is composed of units—individuals—who are organized into sub-systems such as "families," "occupations," and other kinds of institutions. If the individuals in fact participate in the same sociocultural system (SCS), then they are dynamically related, since what happens to some of them will affect the state of some or all of the others. To use terms developed in systems theory, interactions between members of the same *SCS* are governed by constraint. When *A* does or says something to *B*, not *all* responses are open to *B*. If communication has occurred, what *B* does is in some way constrained by what *A* has just done.

Constraint, of course, implies a code imposed on the relationship between *A* and *B*, such that each may interpret the other's behavior more or less accurately. Speech, writing, facial expressions, gestures, semaphore, smoke signals, all have served as codes. Because of culturally patterned constraints, people are able to class some perceptions as the same or similar, and other things as different. All of the social sciences are based on this simple but extremely important fact.

*SCS*s of course have boundaries, though not necessarily geographically contiguous, across which exchanges with the environment occur. For the purposes of this paper, we may consider the environment to include natural habitat and circumjacent *SCS*s. Because these exchanges with the environment occur, an *SCS* can be described as an "open" system. All exchanges between an open system and its environments are dual. Whatever enters the *SCS* must leave it, at some time or another, whether or not its state has been transformed. This sort of dual exchange may be called a throughput, and there are three throughputs of chief concern to us here. The first is that of the units themselves. People enter an *SCS* and sooner or later leave it. They engage in two kinds of environmental exchange: that of matter and energy, and that of information. We may take these one at a time.

Individuals ✓

One of the most important properties of the individual members of an *SCS* is progression through time, or aging.

> We find examples of populations—aggregates of individuals conforming to a common definition—in which individuals are added (born) and subtracted (die) and in which the age of the individual is a relevant and identifiable variable . . . . Population change, both in absolute numbers and in structure, can be discussed in terms of birth and survival functions relating numbers of births and deaths in specific age groups to various aspects of the system . . . . The interaction of populations can be discussed in terms of competitive, complementary, or parasitic relationships among populations of different species, whether the species consist of animals, commodities, social classes, or molecules (Boulding 1968, p. 5).

These statements are true even if relatively simple systems are considered. A simple structure like a clock, for example, even if regularly wound, will not run forever. The parts age and wear away at different rates, and sooner or later some part or sets of parts, will break down and the system will fail unless the parts are replaced. Aging, failure, and replacement of units is as characteristic of cultures as it is of clocks.

Matter and Energy

It is assumed that one of the primary functions of tools and other forms of matter is to increase the efficiency of the SCS in terms of the amount of energy harnessed. The problem of energy has been discussed at length by others (see White 1949, 1959; Sahlins and Service 1960), so this section will focus on the throughput of matter.

The exchange of material with the environment is mediated by technology—the aggregate of tools and techniques directly concerned with getting a living. Technology may be relatively simple, as it is among hunters and gatherers, or extremely complex, as it is among highly industrialized SCSs. Technology is of critical importance in the systemic metaphor because it is an expression of the efficiency of the SCS in adapting to and utilizing its resources. (Mark that we are discussing efficiency of the SCS, not the happiness, contentment, or satisfaction of its members.)

Like many other complex systems, SCSs exhibit a tendency toward growth, an increase in internal complexity. The rate at which such growth occurs is associated with the complexity of the tools and activities used to exploit the environment. Generally speaking, the greater the technological inventory, the more combinations of items are possible, and the more likely it is that the SCS will be characterized by a high rate of technological growth.

The material input is of two types. First, artifactual input consists of tools, buildings, clothing, and other material goods derived from natural substances which are put to use extra-organismically, that is, outside the bodies of the individual members of the SCS. These goods are used and then discarded, either after they have served their purpose or after they have been so worn that it is easier to replace them than to restore them. Different kinds of materials pass through an SCS at different rates: a building is designed to last longer than the candle on a cake. Similarly, the same kinds of artifacts pass through different societies at different rates. An alarm clock will last longer among people living in a cool, dry climate, rather than a hot, moist one. In our own *SCS*, automobiles tend to last longer in rural areas than in urban ones, and this fact is reflected in differential insurance rates. The rates at which artifacts pass through an *SCS* may be referred to as that system's material attrition rate. As an aside, it may be mentioned that the "underdeveloped" economic condition of some societies is partly a function of their high material attrition rate. Where artifactual goods are stolen or quickly destroyed by climate, we may expect that work expended in getting goods that require much productive effort would be dysfunctional. In Samoa, ripe, yellow bananas are highly prized, and banana plants abound, yet Samoans rarely have an opportunity to eat a yellow banana. The reason is that the moment anyone's bananas show signs of ripening, they are begged, confiscated, or stolen by someone else. Thus everyone must eat his bananas while they are still green. Such other "leveling mechanisms" as large feasts, forced loans, expenditure rivalries, and so on, however much they may promote social solidarity, tend to disperse wealth and inhibit its reinvestment (Nash 1966, pp. 35–36). Clearly, the production of material goods depends as much upon the cooperation of other *SCS* members as upon the motivation of the entrepreneur himself.

It is also worth mentioning that a high material attrition rate is also characteristic of industrialized societies with relatively unregulated economies, at least for certain types of artifacts. This is true to the extent that manufacturers profit from the sale of artifacts designed to fall apart on schedule. Production is predicated on the assumption that all artifactual goods will break down, and from the point of view of some of the artisans, the sooner the better. Advertising and "built-in obsolescence" are similarly attempts to maintain a high material attrition rate.

A second type of material input is victual, consisting of food gotten from the environment, consumed and converted into energy, and eliminated. As Cohen (1968, pp. 42–43) observes, the nature of victual input yields some indication of the efficiency of the *SCS*. In many simple and relatively isolated societies, the diet remains monotonously regular throughout the year, or shifts abruptly from one season to the next as one kind of food disappears and another becomes available. Conversely, an efficient *SCS* utilizes trade relationships in such a way that many different types of food are available regardless of season. A less efficient *SCS* can make few dietary substitutions, and its welfare is therefore likely to be bound up with the success of a limited number of highly important food sources. During epidemics, a more differentiated *SCS* is able to substitute another kind of food for one that is no longer available. It is only fair to point out that several technologically simple societies are exceptions to this generalization, for example, some of the Indians of California.

Information

The term "information" is used here broadly, rather than in any mathematical sense. It may be defined as the constraint imposed on any entity in its relations with other entities linked by some communication channel. If communication is to occur, the participants must have corresponding constraints mapped or coded into the system of each (Silverman 1968, p. 150).

Information may enter the *SCS* through innovation or through environmental experience. The information may be of varying utility to the *SCS*. To the extent that it is utile, it may be instrumental—that is, relating to the exchange of matter and energy with the environment—or it may be expressive—that it, ideological, justifying a set of subsistence techniques, enhancing solidarity, or otherwise indirectly promoting durability of the *SCS*.

Information sharing. What happens in the course of data throughput is this: new information appears in the *SCS* and, utile or not, is stored away. In other words, people learn something new and they remember it for a while or they file it away artifactually. The individuals in an *SCS* then constitute data banks, and these banks are periodically scanned by means of processes varying in degree of formality from gossip and visiting to staff meetings and court trials (see Roberts 1964). Much of the information is also transmitted from one person to another so that it comes to be absorbed into the shared informational inventory.

The extent to which any information is shared varies greatly. At one extreme, the data become what Linton has called a "universal," absorbed into a nuclear core of behavioral predispositions, and it may become so characteristic of fully participating adults of that *SCS* that everyone knows it. At the other extreme, the knowledge may be shared by only two or three individuals and deliberately kept secret from others. It is said, for example, that the formula for a popular Italian liqueur is not artifactually stored, is known only to three people, and that these three never travel together so that the formula will not be lost in case of a fatal accident.

There are of course numerous reasons for keeping information secret. At a manifest level, if two *SCS*s are in competition with each other, utile information known to one of them and kept secret from the other will give the knowledgeable *SCS* a competitive advantage. Even if the actual advantage is slight, the fact that the disadvantaged *SCS* suspects that the other controls secret utile information suggests that the disadvantaged *SCS* will need to adopt a more cautious strategy. The same is true for competitive sub-systems within one *SCS*.

Two latent functions of secret information are also apparent. One of these, sub-system differentiation, is analogous to the process called "sharpening" in the psychology of perception. If a sub-system controls information and deliberately keeps it secret from similar sub-systems, it sharpens its own boundaries and pulls its members closer together in a conspiracy of silence. This is a prerequisite for the second latent function: enhancement of sub-system self-image. Secrecy and value are intimately associated in peoples' minds.[3] It is not only that valuable information should be kept secret from members of other sub-systems, but that what is kept secret is itself an expression of what is valuable. Secret handshakes do not help one fraternity to adapt more efficiently than another, but they do acquire a kind of fiat value as a reflection of the brothers' pride in their organization. There are many examples of such expressive information in the ethnographic literature.

---

[3] Of course the valence of secret information may be negative as well as positive in that, if it were generally known, it would discredit the sub-system. Goffman (1963, chap. 2) discusses techniques of controlling such information.

C. A. Valentine provides one illustration in his discussion of ritual among the men of the Lakalai of New Britain:

> All the supplementary mystification which surrounds the masks and the performances not only contributes to masculine pride but heightens the atmosphere of secrecy and the sense of the uncanny as well. Sanctity and taboo further intensify these effects. None but the initiated may handle the masks or witness the transformations from ordinary person to masked man.
>
> Yet virtually the only real secrets beneath all this elaborate cultural camouflage are the details of the internal structures of the masks and the procedures surrounding their construction (Valentine 1961, p. 48).

Goffman makes a similar point: "Often the real secret behind the mystery is that there really is no mystery: the real problem is to prevent the audience from learning this too (Goffman 1959, p. 70)." And other recent works (see Young, 1965) have demonstrated that one of the chief functions of secret information is the expression, maintenance, and enhancement of sub-system solidarity.

Storage and control. The simplest means of storing information is by remembering it. And, in fact, in many *SCS*s lacking a written language, this is one of the few means available, the information being exchanged verbally in face-to-face encounters. This type of transmission—human speech—is characterized by rapid evanescence, or fading; the sound waves which transmit the message are progressively damped by environmental noise until they are no longer detectable.

The use of more complicated methods of information storage involves the encoding of the message into a symbolic arrangement of material elements which evanesces more slowly than speech. In writing, for example, one encodes speech into an arbitrary set of symbols—letters, say—and organizes certain materials—pen and ink—in such a way that the information contained in the letters is represented on paper. As long as this arrangement of elements lasts, the information in the letters may be read by anyone with access to the same set of coded constraints the writer is using. This is true of all techniques of artifactual storage. Data is first encoded, then this code is imposed on a set of material elements in the form of a stable arrangement of parts, whether the parts be letters on paper, oxide molecules on magnetic tape, or notches on a stick; then, during the process of retrieval, the message is decoded and put to use.

All stored information involves a stable arrangement of elements and, conversely, all stable states constitute stored information, in the sense that they are records of past events. Historical geologists, for example, occupy themselves with attempts to decode the information stored systematically in the various layers of the earth's crust. Archaeologists in some areas use dendro-chronological techniques based on information stored in the growth rings of tree trunks. All such interpretations of non-random arrangements depend upon our ability to determine the constraints imposed by one event upon a succeeding one. Presumably, too, "remembering" involves a stable arrangement of physical structures within the brain.

Even without artifactual storage, the amount of information in any given *SCS* is likely to be more than the sum of the information controlled by the individual members of the *SCS*. The pieces of information controlled by individuals often fit together like pieces of a jigsaw puzzle. Each worker on an assembly line may know only enough to perform his limited task, but together the workers constitute a production unit.

One of the more obvious consequences of elaborate techniques for the artifactual storage of information is that the individual himself becomes less important as a storage cell. In non-Western societies one of the functions of old people is remembering such things as old legends, myths, and ethical principles, and they are frequently consulted on these matters. As Elliot (1886, pp. 170–71) described the situation among the Aleuts, neighbors of the Eskimo in the northern Pacific:

> Before the advent of Russian priests, every village had one or two old men at least, who considered it their especial business to educate the children; thereupon, in the morning or the evening, when all were at home, these aged teachers would seat themselves in the center of one of the largest village yourts or "oolagmuh": the young folks surrounded them, and listened attentively to what they said— sometimes failing memory would cause the old preceptors to repeat over and over again the same advice or legend in the course of a lecture. The respect of the children, however, never allowed or occasioned an interruption of such a senile oration.

Such were the conditions among at least one non-literate society a century ago. A further perusal of the ethnographic literature suggests the proposition that when writing appears among a people characterized by a low rate of literacy, and when books and other archives are rare, artifactual storage of information does not necessarily replace the oldsters but rather supplements their memories. Usually the first written records to appear in a predominantly non-literate society are sacred writings and records of economic transactions. Access to these archives tends to be controlled by a class of specially educated persons, who may or may not be priests, and who are frequently older than the general population. The members of this educated class then transmit such information to the lay people as they deem wise. This sort of arrangement persisted in Europe until less than 500 years ago when, with the spread of the printing press, esoteric information became vulgarized. This, in fact, suggests the origin of the university lecture system, developed at a time when books were hand-printed and so rare that they were read aloud before the class by professor–priests.

In industrialized societies, what mythology remains important to the SCS is written down, printed, and sold in bookstores. The world's best seller is the Bible; more than one and a half billion copies have appeared since 1800, in 1,280 languages. Such improved storage devices render older people redundant as consultants and arbitrators.[4]

Scanning procedures retrieve and apply relevant utile information. Information that is not utile disappears from the system more rapidly, either because the people who know it forget it, or because they themselves die. Given a long enough period of time and the existence of SCS change, all data eventually become useless and disappear from the system. These processes of storing, scanning, and retrieving information are examined in a paper by Roberts (1964), which applies the concepts to an analysis of the political development of several American Indian societies.

The criteria by which information is judged utile or not are the quantity and nature of the material and energy input of the system, the technology that affects it, the expressive information that facilitates it, and the cumulative impact of these subsistence-

---

[4] There is a story, possibly apocryphal, of a society whose ritual included a complex rain dance, the details of which were memorized by elders. Over time interest in the dance waned and, one by one, the elders died. When an unusually severe draught encouraged the members of the society to try the dance again, they found they had no consultants left alive. Their solution was to consult a book written by an anthropologist years before, which contained a description of the dance.

related activities on the relationships between component sub-systems.

In principle, it might be said, all of the information that any system could possibly use is being transmitted from the environment. The kind and amount of "absolute information" (Brillouin 1968, p. 162) received, however, is determined by the arrangement of the *SCS*s parts. The arrangement of parts generates a distinctive external orientation, or set of constraints, within the *SCS*. In a sense, the *SCS* operates here in a way analogous to that of a radio receiver. In wireless communications, a transmitter sends out a message through the air and a radio receives and decodes it. Within the broadcast band, the air may be full of electromagnetic waves from various transmitters operating on different frequencies. A single-channel receiver, however, can be tuned to only one frequency out of many and so necessarily selects and decodes only a few out of the many possible messages. The frequency to which the receiver is tuned is determined entirely by the arrangement of, and relationships between, its component parts. Similarly an *SCS* can absorb only a select few out of many possible "messages" in its environment. In our own *SCS*, for example, the natural habitat—the water, the air, the biota—has for years been yielding evidence that "something is wrong," particularly in and near urban areas. Yet, given our idea that progress is good and that it means "conquering nature," and that this, in turn, involves polluting our environment, our survival for another century remains problematic. It may be that our *SCS* is so critically "tuned" to the message it will receive and act upon that we are in the position of the parasitic micro-organism which proved so highly efficient that it doomed itself by killing its host.

It is worth suggesting that the existence in any *SCS* of people controlling information of little value to others may still contribute to the overall adaptability of the *SCS*, because currently worthless information may some day *become* utile as the *SCS* changes. To the extent that an *SCS* lacks inutile information, it resembles a highly specialized organism which is maximally efficient but extremely dependent on a specific configuration of environmental elements.[5]

---

[5] Similar generalizations were expressed by Sahlins and Service (1960) as the "law of evolutionary potential," and by Ashby (1956) as the "law of requisite variety."

The existence in an *SCS* of people whose knowledge is of little or no utility to others means that the *SCS* is still generalized to a degree and that, should there be a drastic alteration in the rate or direction of *SCS* change, the knowledge they control may mean the difference between survival and extinction for the total system. At the same time, while it is true that knowledge that was never previously utile may become utile, it is perhaps less likely that knowledge rendered inutile may ever regain its previous value. Information related to obsolete occupational skills, for example, will probably remain inutile, and it is unfortunate for the aged that they so often act as storage units for this sort of information. Occupations are linked to technology and, in this sense, *SCS* change is largely irreversible.

Matching of inputs and SCS components. From a conceptual perspective, the information storage units are not individuals but rather the roles occupied by individuals. This is so because the informational inventory consists of that knowledge to which members of an *SCS* have access, either directly (by remembering it) or indirectly (through scanning of data banks), and informational access, and the capacity to process that information, are functions of the roles people occupy. Indeed, it is possible to disregard the role structure too, and an approach has been developed by Roberts (1951, 1956, 1961, 1964) which views as information all of what is usually defined as "culture."

All extant *SCS*s are in a constant state of change, so it is not possible to assume that any given system is in a "steady state." We may nevertheless assume that there is at least a modicum of congruence in the nature of the three inputs. That is to say, the structure of roles formed by individuals within the *SCS* must involve storage of such information as will enable the system as a whole to adapt to external circumstances, maintain the throughput of material and energy, and survive. From the point of view of the individual, this means that he must learn enough of the right kinds of information to enable him to make a living and get along with neighbors and kinsmen in his given *SCS* context.

Aging

Let us assume that an individual's personality reflects the information he has acquired so far in his life, and that the most influential and enduring information is that which was acquired in the years leading to maturity. The validity of this proposition is debatable—certainly learning occurs throughout one's life—but it is a commonly accepted one in the behavioral sciences, and it certainly seems true of many kinds of animals as well. Zoo keepers tell us that, not only can't you teach an old dog new tricks, but you can't teach an old lion either. As Hediger (1964, p. 27) observes in the case of captured wild animals:

> The transplanted animal's behavior may be of two different kinds, depending on its origin or the new locality. The second kind is usually seen in the undeveloped still adaptable young wild animal; it may fit the new environment and settle down to it. The first kind on the other hand occurs with the older wild animal already set in its ways and rigidly conditioned by its previous background. It has lost its plasticity and adaptability, and so must behave as it always has done. True, such individuals may often be kept in captivity for a time, but they never become properly adapted to the new situation. If they survive capture they usually linger in a chronic state of excitement generally caused by their uneasiness in the presence of man, and with a basically rigid attitude of mind, so to speak. This prevents any suitable treatment, even the taking of food; it may result in nervous disturbances, reduce resistence to disease and lead to death, psychologically caused.

The existence of such changes among human beings has received some empirical support. (Lieberman 1961; Camargo and Preston 1945).

On the whole, the aged tend to be the more stable and conservative members of any *SCS*. Of course, it is not necessary that the aged actually change through time and become more conservative, but they may stay pretty much the same while the *SCS* changes. This is probably not a merely contemporary phenomenon. Two thousand years ago, Aristotle was complaining about the recklessness and disobedience of the young. And around the world, the aged seem to be the guardians of the old traditions. Alland (1968, p. 219) calls this the result of "learning fixation," and Riley and Foner (1968, p. 5) summarize a number of recent findings in this way:

> In general, older people are more conservative than younger people in their political ideology. . . . Age appears to contribute for better or for worse, to the stability of the social structure.

Given these assumptions, we have then a situation in which an old person dies in an *SCS* and a new individual is born and replaces him. This person in turn grows up, learning as he grows, until he becomes a fully participating adult, displaying relatively fixed values and behavioral predispositions. He too gradually becomes old and dies. And his death is actually an essential part of social life, as was the death of the aged person he replaced. Aside from the problem of population control, there are other difficulties in managing too long-lived a population. Boulding (1970) describes one of them this way:

> [Immortality] . . . . would present the human race with probably the greatest crisis it has ever had to face. Who, for instance, would want to be an assistant professor for 500 years? What makes life tolerable, especially for the young, is death.

Then too, if the behavior of the older person is relatively conservative and fixed, the replacement of old people by changeable young enhances the adaptability of the SCS and thus increases its chances for survival.

It is clear that the information one acquires during his growth years will remain utile for the remainder of his life if there is little or no change in the environment of his SCS. If learning initially was utile, and if nothing else changes, then it stays utile, no matter how old he becomes.

On the other hand, to the extent that environmental change takes place, the slower-changing information controlled by the older individual becomes of less adaptive utility to the SCS and ultimately becomes inutile. A high rate of environmental change generates a high rate of sociocultural change because of the SCSs tendency to adapt itself and survive. Faced with a highly mutative technology and set of values, the older person clings to those skills and beliefs he learned in his youth. In other words, as part of the total system, older persons represent banks of inutile data and the information they control, whether instrumental or expressive, is of little utility to the rest of society. The congruence between what they know and what the SCS needs to know in order to adapt is lessened.

Over time, all systems as complex as an SCS tend to maximize the storage and retrieval of utile information because rewards ordinarily accrue to those people occupying roles whose function it is to ensure the adaptive efficiency of the SCS through the control and application of utile information, either instrumental or expressive. In other words, the man who knows how to hunt successfully, and the shaman who knows more about the treatment of disease, is likely to be better off than the mediocre hunter or the unknown shaman. The aged and any others whose information is of little utility tend not to be rewarded. And as their material welfare declines, they develop a parasitic relationship with the other members of the *SCS*.

It may be argued that many aged and infirm people are well provided for by their children, even in societies characterized by a high rate of institutional change. They may be shown a great deal of respect, so that this generalization lacks credibility. Children support their parents, whether the parents know anything of value or not. It can be pointed out, however, that within the context of the family—a sub-system of the total *SCS*—aged persons may control information that is utile in the *expressive* sense. They may repeat anecdotes about family ancestors, explain kinship networks, serve as instructors in ritual esoterica, and in other ways contribute information that lends historical depth to the family and enhances its survival as a corporate unit.

The situation that is historically normal in industrialized *SCS*s, of course, is that only the aged, who control obsolete information, and the young, who do not control enough exploitable information, are devalued. But it is possible to imagine an *SCS* in which the rate of institutional change is so rapid that not only is the information controlled by the aged quickly rendered unexploitable, but also the information controlled by the fully participating adults. One of the requirements of social life is that there must be continuity enough in the demands of the role structure to permit people to be prepared and recruited into appropriate roles.

In terms more consistent with the systemic model we have been using, we might point out that as one increases the amount and rate of information input, errors increase, too, until asymptote is reached, a point at which the channel capacity of the system is exceeded. From our own experience we know that it is easy to drive a car along a country road, where we can easily handle the few novel circumstances that arise. We know also that it seems to take more energy to drive through city traffic or on a crowded freeway, where the rate and kinds of novel information input are great, and where we are more likely to make a driving error. And we can imagine a situation in which we are surrounded by many other vehicles moving quickly and erratically, their drivers sharing with us no set of mutual constraints. In such a situation we would not be able to drive at all because we would be unable to receive and process quickly enough all of the novel information with which we were being bombarded.

There is no reason to suppose that SCSs may not be subject to similar limits. Margaret Mead's second study of the Village of Pere (1956) suggests that some of these limits may be broader than we have thought, and that some SCSs can adapt to changing circumstances rather readily. On the other hand, we have the experience of many American Indian societies, where environmental change occurred at such a rapid rate that the established adaptive mechanisms of the society were unable to handle it. Thus, the SCS itself lost its integrative quality, and the population failed to reproduce itself (see Bohannan and Plog 1967).

At the other end of the continuum of SCS change rates, we might imagine a society in which the rate of change was so nearly nil that the individual accumulation of utile information was an ordinal process and, were all other things equal, the person of most value to society would be the one who had lived the longest. If the control of utile information were associated with political power, the gerontocracy that would result might not be so far from the kind of social structure that exists among the Tiwi of Australia (although for different reasons—Hart and Pilling 1960), or possibly, judging from archeological evidence, the aboriginal population of some parts of California (Olson 1930, pp. 192–93)— or perhaps Shangri La!

The preceding statements suggest some of the reasons why the aged are generally devalued in industrialized SCSs, which are usually characterized by a rapid rate of institutional change and by elaborate means of artifactual information storage.

It should not be thought, incidentally, that in referring to industrialized SCSs, we mean to include all those which are socially complex; that is, those with a high population density, cities of considerable size, a complicated division of labor, and so forth. The operative concept here is the substitution of machines for men in subsistence-getting activities. There are likely to be significant differences in the rates of institutional change in complex societies with peasant-based economies and in societies as industrialized as those of Europe and North America. Far too little quantitative comparative work has been done in the area, but Kalish (1969, p. 85) asked a group of about two dozen Cambodian students, coming from a complex but largely agrarian society, whether:

> . . . given the necessity of choice, they would save the life of their mother, their wife, or their daughter. All responded immediately that they would save their mother, and their .tone implied that only an immoral or ignorant person would even ask such a question. [Kalish doubts] whether 10% of a comparable American group would give that response.

Kastenbaum (1964) asked a group of American nurses how much effort they would expend in saving the life of a twenty-year old, an eighty-year old, and a pet dog. The results showed that the lives were ranked in an expectable order of importance—twenty-year old, eighty-year old, and pet dog—but it is interesting that the difference between the twenty-year old and the eighty-year old was greater than the difference between the eighty-year old and the dog.

Of course, a high rate of SCS change is not the only condition under which the aged may be treated poorly. Devaluation can occur under other conditions as well. In industrialized SCSs we see it because the older person is not able to change the information he controls rapidly enough to keep up with the changing needs of the SCS, but among certain hunting and gathering societies, characterized by simple technology and enforced geographic mobility under harsh environmental circumstances, it may occur simply because the older person is not able physically to keep up with the others as they move around in their search for food. Such conditions are found among the Sirionó of the Bolivian rain forest, for example.

> Since status is determined largely by immediate utility to the group, the inability of the aged to compete with the younger members of the society places them somewhat in the category of excess baggage. Having outlived their usefulness they are relegated to a position of obscurity. Actually the aged are quite a burden. They eat but are unable to hunt, fish, or collect food; they sometimes hoard a young spouse, but are unable to beget children; they move at a snail's pace and hinder the mobility of the group. . . . When a person becomes too ill or infirm to follow the fortunes of the band, he is abandoned to shift for himself (Holmberg 1969, pp. 224–25).

To put this in other terms, we may suggest that there are some SCSs that exist under such a set of environmental circumstances that they must travel about frequently or rapidly in order to maintain the throughput of victual material. Here, if there is little SCS change going on, the aged may control utile information; however, the inventory is small enough so that much of his information is shared by others. The aged person then becomes redundant and he may be physically sacrificed because he hampers the quest of his fellows for food or water. It is important to understand that it is not redundancy alone which leads to his abandonment or sacrifice. A certain amount of redundancy or repetition is functional in a communication system because it reduces the likelihood of errors during transmission and inadvertent loss. Rather, the redundancy of the aged person makes possible his abandonment, though it is by no means a sufficient cause. It should also be pointed out that these generalizations do not apply to all hunting and gathering societies, some of whom have considerable leisure time and ample food for their non-productive oldsters, as recent work has demonstrated (Lee and DeVore 1968; Lee 1969). This sort of of treatment of the aged, killing or abandonment, may suggest that in societies where it occurs the aged are dealt with contemptuously. This is not necessarily the case, as we shall see.

In any case, one may note a paradoxical effect here. In relatively simple societies under relatively harsh environmental conditions, the rate of *SCS* change, and subsequently the tempo of informational obsolescence, may be low, but the successful integration of the elderly into society depends a great deal on physical strength, or at least endurance, of which the aged have little. In other words, they may control utile information but are not strong enough to adapt to the demands of their surroundings. In industrialized societies, on the other hand, more efficient tools and a more complex division of labor make work less dependent on physical strength, but a highly developed technology means a high rate of *SCS* change so that the elderly become more or less rapidly obsolete as parts of the man-machine system.

Summary

We know that the status and treatment of the aged vary greatly from one society to another. In those societies where they are killed or abandoned, as among some hunters and gatherers, the aged may or may not have relatively high status up to the point of death. On the other hand, we have suggested that where *SCS* change is rapid, either because the society is undergoing, or has undergone, industrialization, or because of culture contact with a more dominant, complex society, the information controlled by the aged becomes rapidly obsolete. This high rate of informational obsolence is reflected in a decline in their social participation. The low incidence of social participation in turn contributes to their loss of status.

More specifically, we propose that societies may be ranked in terms of the degree of participation of their aged members in social life, this participation being made possible, of course, by their control of utile information. It is also proposed that societies may be ranked in terms of the status accorded to their aged. Finally, it is hypothesized that, inasmuch as a person is socially valuable largely because of his knowledge, which is reflected in what he does, the status of the aged should vary directly with their participation in the social life of the community.

METHODS AND RESULTS

It remains for us to give some empirical substance to the general propositions presented in the foregoing discussion. Attempting to build on the efforts of Simmons, we made use of the Human Relations Area Files (HRAF). The HRAF is a collection of ethnographic materials already coded into such categories as "dancing," "visiting and hospitality," "community structure," and so on. This information is coded separately for each of the nearly 200 societies in the HRAF, an arrangement which greatly facilitates cross-cultural research. But because of the inherent limitations of the HRAF as a research tool, various constraints were imposed on the nature of the hypotheses that could be formulated and the kinds of procedures that could be employed in the analysis of the data.

This is not the place to deal with the technical problems involved in large scale cross-cultural research. With varying degrees of success in wrestling with the many difficulties, a considerable literature in comparative methodology already exists, not only in anthropology but in several related disciplines.[6] It should be mentioned, however, that the problem is compounded in the present instance because of the previously mentioned paucity of data on the aged in the ethnographic corpus. Thus, it is necessary to consider this initial attempt more as a pilot study than a definitive

[6] A good overview of the main methodological problems can be obtained from Whiting (1968).

exegesis wherein the demands of adequate sampling procedures and attention to carefully defined units of analysis have been properly satisfied.

The systems theoretical approach adopted here requires that the aged be viewed as one of several subsets in an *SCS* which is capable, in varying degrees, of receiving, processing, and transmitting information, and furthermore, that any understanding of the treatment of the aged must be seen as a consequence of the internal arrangement of informational resources available to a particular *SCS*. Our previous discussion has indicated some of the conditions which affect the role of the aged as sources of information relevant to the larger society. Our problem now is to specify how this position of the elderly with respect to their capacity to process information determines the kind of treatment they receive within the system as a whole.

The hypothesis to be tested states that the esteem in which the aged are held in a given society varies directly with the degree of control they maintain over the society's informational resources. By esteem we refer to the whole complex of behavioral traits manifested by the members of the society in treating the aged insofar as this treatment maintains the latter's integrity and worth as a subset of the *SCS*. Although the precise operational definition is somewhat problematic, it seems clear that the aged are recognized in all *SCS*s as a distinct category (see Linton 1942). Thus, each *SCS* must make some choice as to the manner in which it will deal with the aged as a social configuration, from veneration at one extreme to contempt at the other.

The variable of informational control refers to the amount of information processed by the aged relative to the total informational pool available to the *SCS*. The categories of informational control proposed by Roberts would be ideally suited for operationalizing this variable. Unfortunately, such a procedure demands too much of the kind of data available in the ethnographic literature. Thus, an alternative method was used to tap this variable. But, before outlining these operational details, it is necessary to state the general methodological procedures used in this study.

After perusing the data available in the HRAF, it was decided that the most productive way to proceed initially was to use as a sample all the societies for which there were relatively detailed descriptive data filed under the categories relevant to the treatment of the aged. Using the files housed at City University of New York, coders collected data from a pool of some 30 societies judged to be adequate for the task. Protocols were developed on four variables—*informational control among the aged, treatment of the aged, rate of institutional change, and ecological factors affecting the aged.* The last two variables will not be treated systematically in this paper, but will be dealt with subsequently in a more extensive examination of this general problem.

From the original pool of societies protocols were completed for 26 cases. The distribution of this sample ranges well over the major ethnographic regions of the world: East Eurasia 8, North America 6, Africa 4, Circum-Mediterranean 4, Insular Pacific 2, and South America 2. Furthermore, no two cases share the same sampling province as specified by Murdock (1968). And lastly, the sample covers a variety of cultural types, including hunters and gatherers, pastoralists, horticulturalists, peasants, and several societies with a mixed economic base.

With respect to the independent variable, informational control, data were coded on the role played by the aged in social situations along two dimensions. First, each instance was coded for the relevant aspect of culture content involved, i.e., political, economic, ideological, and so on. Second, and more importantly for our purpose, each instance was coded for one of five informational processes involving the aged in terms of (1) participating in situations, such as feasts, games, or visiting groups; (2) consulting; (3) making decisions; (4) entertaining; or (5) arbitrating. Before the coding procedures had gotten very far, it was found necessary to add a sixth category, that of teaching. It can be demonstrated that these informational process categories form an unidimensional variable of increasing levels of elaboration, thus this pool of six items may reasonably be considered a measure of informational control available to the aged.

Using the sample of 26 societies, an attempt was made to construct a Guttman scale for both dimensions of the informational control variable. Whiting, one of the most knowledgeable anthropologists in the area of cross-cultural studies, has recently judged the scaling of cultural features the most elegant method of measurement in comparative research (1968, p. 714). Of course, not all data can be subjected to this sort of scrutiny and ordered elegantly. For example, various kinds of scaling procedures were applied to the first dimension of information control discussed above, i.e., content categories, but the intransigence of the data prevailed. No reasonable pattern could be constructed among the various aspects of culture. It would appear that more information is required before such concepts as politics, religion, economics, and so on, can be related to the function of the aged within a comparative framework.

Nevertheless, the dimension of informational process proved appropriate for the unidimensional, cumulative ordering inherent in Guttman scaling. Tables 1 and 2 present the scalogram and scale developed from the six items of informational process. A '1' indicates presence of the item, a '0', absence; an 'A', presence of the item with an error in the scale type, and 'B', absence, with

TABLE 1
Scalogram of informational control among the aged

		1	2	3	4	5	6
I.	Bali	1	1	1	1	1	1
	Bushman	1	1	1	1	1	1
	Monguor	1	1	1	1	1	1
	Ainu	1	1	1	1	1	1
	China	1	1	1	A	1	1
	Rural Irish	1	1	1	1	A	1
	Navaho	1	1	A	1	A	1
II.	Korea	1	1	1	1	1	0
	Tiv	1	1	1	1	1	0
	Kikuyu	1	1	1	A	1	0
III.	Chukchee	1	1	1	1	0	0
	Gond	1	1	A	1	0	0
	Mandan	1	1	A	1	0	0
	Ifugao	1	1	A	1	0	0
IV.	Tallensi	1	1	1	0	0	0
	Serbs	1	1	1	0	0	0
	Lapps	1	1	1	0	0	0
	Ojibwa	1	1	1	0	0	0
	Micmac	1	1	1	0	0	0
	Inca	1	1	1	0	0	B
V.	Gilyak	1	1	0	0	0	0
	Siriono	A	1	0	0	0	0
VI.	Rewala	1	0	0	0	0	0
	Nahane (Kaska)	1	0	0	0	0	0
	Western Tibet	1	0	0	0	B	0
	Aleut	1	0	0	0	0	B

Total $N = 26$; Coefficient of Scalability $= .74$

an error in the scale type. The coefficient of scalability, as developed by Menzel (1953) was used in preference to the coefficient of reproducibility as the former corrects for extreme marginals. Since the measure is more demanding, it tends to produce weaker values than would be obtained by the use of the coefficient of reproducibility. In this case the scale attains a value of .74, which is reasonably above the suggested level of acceptance, somewhere between .60 and .65.

TABLE 2
Scale of informational control among the aged

Step Number	Informational Process	Proportion of Sample Discriminated	Errors
1	Participating	100	1
2	Consulting	84	0
3	Decision-making	77	4
4	Entertaining	54	2
5	Arbitrating	38	3
6	Teaching	27	2

One somewhat surprising result is that entertaining proved to be a higher scale step than decision-making. It could well be that not sufficient attention has been given to the function of entertainment as a way of processing information in an SCS. Certainly, it should give pause when a recent national survey among American high school students found that Bob Hope is among the top three mentioned as the individual most admired! With few exceptions, such as Freud's work on joking and various papers on games by Roberts and his associates (e.g. Roberts and Sutton-Smith 1962), this dimension of cultural content has been sadly neglected. Our data suggest that this whole area requires greater consideration.

We now turn to the dependent variable in our hypothesis, the treatment of the aged. In order to tap the empirical richness of this variable, a protocol with 24 items was used by coders to extract as much of the behavioral diversity as possible. This included such items (all with reference to the aged) as: special place or sitting arrangements; geographical separation; food privileges; special costumes, ornamentation, or body marks; deferential greetings, verbal or gestural; exclusive decoration or grooming by others; generalized fear and avoidance by others; abandonment to the elements/animals; and physically assaulted and killed, or sacrificed. Most of the items had either a positive or a negative valence with respect to the integrity of the aged. However, a few items could have had either valence depending on the context in which they occurred.

Because the treatment of the aged variable does not lend itself to the more demanding Guttman scaling technique, an alternative procedure was used based on a ratio of the positive and negative items available on the protocols. Thus, for each of the 24 items for which it was possible to have information, each code was judged to be either positive—reflecting the high esteem in which the aged are held—or negative—reflecting disdain for the aged. A score was then obtained by subtracting the number of negative items from the positive ones and dividing by the total number of items, in this case, 24.

Of couse, the data available on each society did not yield information on all 24 items. Because of the influence of this factor on the rating technique, societies which are poorly reported, and thus have fewer total items coded, tend to have slightly deflated scores. Nevertheless, this technique proved to be the most realistic solution to the knotty problem of the discrepancy in the amount of data available for the analysis. Since all of the societies in the sample were considered to have relatively thorough coverage of the aged, it is somewhat more probable that if the item were present it would have been reported by the ethnographer.

TABLE 3

Scale of treatment of the aged

I.	China	.79	V.	Tiv	.16
	Bushmen	.62		Lapps	.16
	Monguor	.62		Chukchee	.12
	Navaho	.50		Ojibwa	.12
				Gilyak	.12
II.	Bali	.42	VI.	Korea	.08
				Gond	.08
				Aleut	.08
III.	Ainu	.33		Mandan	.04
	Rural Irish	.33		Micmac	.04
	Tallensi	.33		Rewala	.04
			VII.	Sirionó	.00
IV.	Serbs	.29		Ifugao	− .04
	Inca	.25		Western Tibet	− .12
	Kikuyu	.20		Nahane (Kaska)	− .12

The rating scale for the treatment of the aged is shown on Table 3. The higher the score, the greater the esteem enjoyed by the aged. For the purpose of subsequent calculations, the scale is arbitrarily divided into seven equal segments, with the exception of the extremes where a somewhat broader range of scores is collapsed together.

The distribution of societies in Table 3 confirms one of the propositions discussed earlier which states the conditions under which the aged are devalued. Taking into account only the bottom three levels of the scale, 80 percent of the societies are nomadic during at least part of the annual cycle. On the other hand, only one case (9 percent) among the top four levels of the scale is a nomadic society. The aged among the Bushmen enjoy a very high esteem despite the fact that this is a society continually moving about seeking sustenance from the inhospitable Kalahari Desert. Furthermore, this high level of esteem continues to operate even though those aged who are unable to maintain the mobility imposed upon the group must occasionally be abandoned. Although it is true that, with the exception of the Bushmen, all the societies in our sample that abandon and/or assault and kill their aged also score in the lower half of the scale, Koty (1933) provides ample evidence that these extreme measures are not necessarily associated with low esteem. Indeed, of the five cases in our sample where the aged are physically assaulted and killed—among the Chuckchee, Lapps, Ojibwa, Ifugao and Micmac—there is clear evidence in at least the first three cases that this measure is only taken when requested by the elderly victim himself. Given the scale distribution of those societies where such extreme treatment categories are found, it appears that our measure of esteem was sufficiently sensitive to take account of these ethnographic facts.

It is now possible to consider the test of the hypothesis regarding the relationship between informational control and the treatment of the aged. The data from Tables 1 and 3 were used to calculate a measure of association. It is worth noting that each of these scales were constructed by judges working independently of each other, thus avoiding one possible source of contamination. The measure of association used to relate the two scales is the Gamma coefficient, which has been judged to be the most easily interpretable for the analysis of ordinal scale data.[7] The correlation of the two scales attains a Gamma value of .685 (p < .01), thus giving relatively strong support for the hypothesis that the control of various informational processes among the aged will predict the degree of esteem they enjoy within a particular society.

DISCUSSION

We have, first of all, developed a scale of informational control among the aged people of 26 societies, which represents an "opportunistic sample" of the many societies available in the HRAF. The six items of the scale were found to be unidimensional, with the items running from most common to least common: (1) participating in social situations; (2) consulting; (3) decision-making; (4) entertaining; (5) arbitrating; and (6) teaching. Secondly, we scored each of the 26 societies for treatment of their aged, based on the presence or absence of 24 traits dealing with the behavior of other members of the SCS towards old people. (Expectedly, China was at the top of the positive end.) Finally, we demonstrated an association between the two scales which, within the limits of the experimental design and procedures used, seems to indicate that the degree of control that the aged manifest over utile information does determine to some extent their treatment in the SCS.

The last finding, that high informational control among the aged is associated with their being held in esteem, will startle few who are familiar with previous cross-cultural efforts. This, after all, is part of the import of Simmons' book. Generalizing from his perusal of the literature, he states:

> Even though the aged have had to withdraw from the rigors of life and betake themselves to domestic shelter, they have not been entirely doomed to passivity. The aged have not been mere social parasites. By the exercise of their knowledge, wisdom, experience, property rights, and religious or magical powers they have often played useful roles (1945, p. 216).

Such a brief treatment of the subject as we have presented here raises more issues than it solves. We will make seven problems explicit in unordered fashion.

It became clear in the course of this preliminary investigation that Simmons was right in stating that there were indeed vast

---

[7] See Costner (1965). In this article, Costner shows that Gamma better meets the requirements as a measure of association if the criterion is the "proportional reduction in error of estimation" made possible by the relationship. Gamma fulfills this criterion better than other rank correlation methods, such as Kendall's *Tau* and Spearman's *Rho*.

differences in the treatment of the aged according to sex. His suggested determinant, the organization of the family, however, is not really satisfactory, for several reasons. If it is true that old men have relatively higher status in strongly patrilineal, or generally male-oriented societies, like the Chinese, and conversely, old women are held in relatively high esteem in matrilineal, or female-oriented societies, like the Navaho, one nevertheless finds himself wondering why some societies are patrilineal and others matrilineal in the first place. Moreover, a case could be made for strong lineality being a result of differential esteem, rather than a cause.

The last critical comment, that correlations do not prove causality, could be made of this paper or, in fact, almost any other synchronic, comparative study, though in the present case hopefully with somewhat less force. Dealing as one does with the static, descriptive data of the HRAF, it is difficult to demonstrate the direction of causility, but it is not impossible if, for example, one is able to trace the thread back to climatic variables (see Whiting 1964; Maxwell 1967) or if one adopts certain logico-statistical techniques suggested by Blalock (1964). Alternatively, of course, if one had available complete historical data for a number of societies, one might then establish the temporal sequence of changes in the independent and dependent variables.

In a similar vein, we feel that the correlation presented earlier between informational control and esteem has not gone far enough. We have suggested that rapid institutional change, which is characteristic of industrialized SCSs as well as others in situations of intense culture contact, generates a high rate of informational obsolescence and thus leads to the devaluation of the aged. The link between rapid SCS change and loss of informational control for the aged remains to be demonstrated.

In association with the tempo of SCS change, certain other factors undoubtedly assert themselves. In some SCSs, as our own, the rapidity of SCS change seems partly a result of the complexity of the extant informational inventory. The more items in the inventory, the more combinations are possible and the more likely they are to be made. On the other hand, it is obvious that what are generally called ecological variables are also at work, in our own society as well as others. Such conditions as population density, availability of resources, climate, ease of transport, and community locations favorable or inimical to trade with other peoples, are all important as determinants of the tempo of *SCS* change. And these are all aside from the direct impact of the environment on the ability of a population to support non-productive old people.

The limits of the social category "old person" vary greatly from place to place. In some societies, a man may be considered "old" when he becomes a grandfather, which may be in his 40th year. Or the ethnographer himself may be the judge of who is old and who is not. And we have not drawn any distinction in this study between people who are merely old and people who are decrepit. This is not because the distinction is unimportant, but because it is so seldom made in the ethnographic literature. It is interesting to consider the position of the decrepit in, say, a society in which old people are held in great esteem. On the one hand, the response of the other *SCS* members is subject to generalization from more powerful and respected elders to their disoriented and enfeebled fellows.

On the other hand, if it is true, as we have suggested, that esteem is determined by control of utile information, then the decrepit aged are indeed socially bankrupt. The balance between the two forces must be a nice one, and if we are thinking in terms of something like compassion towards the aged, the truly decrepit provide a more critical test than the merely "old."

During the investigation, it was apparent that, although the content categories of informational control, i.e., political, economic, social, religious, and so on, could not be subjected to unidimensional scaling, nevertheless the distinction in each category between instrumental and expressive information was of little importance. The relationship of the variables appears to hold regardless of whether the information being processed is instrumental or expressive, certainly a point worth pursuing in future research.

A final observation is that the model presented here is really too simple. We have already discussed the importance of ecological factors and the rate of institutional change in the *SCS*, but in addition there are certainly other informational variables which should be taken into account as possible intervening factors affecting the predicted relationship. We may mention merely one such consideration: linguistic homogeneity–heterogeneity. Like Russian and Spanish, the English language is relatively homogeneous. It is bifurcated only into Commonwealth or North American dialects. Other languages, like Chinese, are broken into several mutually nearly unintelligible dialects. And at the other extreme, as in some parts of Africa, dialects may be separated only by a few villages. Linguistic heterogeneity–homogeneity is of enormous importance to people in terms of trade, transport, solidarity, and other aspects of social and economic relationships, and for its deliberate exchange of utile information! There are surely other such informational variables yet to be considered, or even recognized.

These theoretical and methodological points have been brought up here not in order to vitiate the results of the present study but rather to delineate some problem areas for further research. Indeed the findings presented here represent only part of the data collected from the HRAF, and we expect to devote more attention to these and other problems in the future. Cross-national studies of aging have been facilitated by the existence of archives, and if the large-scale cross-cultural approach, taking into account primitive as well as technologically advanced societies, has in the past been hampered by skimpy or uneven data, one feels nevertheless that with the ongoing diffusion of effective medical care and the increasing articulation of simple societies with national forms of government, perhaps the cross-cultural study of aging will become somewhat more significant as a heuristic technique. Ours is, after all, but one of many thousands of societies in the world. And each society is, in a sense, a self-contained experiment in the handling of older people. Each is searching for a solution to a social problem that all of them face.

REFERENCES

Alland, A. 1967. *Evolution and human behavior*. Garden City: Natural History Press.

Arensberg, C. M., & Kimball, S. T. 1940. *Family and community in Ireland*. Cambridge: Harvard Univ. Press.

Ashby, W. R. 1956. *An introduction to cybernetics*. London: Chapman and Hall.

Blalock, H. M. 1964. *Causal inferences in non-experimental research*. Chapel Hill: Univ. of North Carolina Press.

Bohannan, P., & Plog, F. 1967. *Beyond the frontier*. Garden City: Natural History Press.

Boulding, K. E. 1968. General systems theory—The skeleton of a science. In *Modern systems research for the behavioral scientist*, ed. W. Buckley. Chicago: Aldine.

Boulding, K. E. 1970. Ecology and environment. In *Social science in the schools: A search for a rationale*, ed. I. Morrisset & W. W. Stevens, Jr. New York: Holt, Rinehart, & Winston.

Brillouin, L. 1968. Thermodynamics and information theory. In *Modern systems research for the behavioral scientist*, ed. W. Buckley. Chicago: Aldine.

Bromley, D. 1966. *The psychology of human aging*. Harmondsworth: Penguin.

Camargo, O., & Preston, G. H. 1945. What happens to patients who are hospitalized for the first time when over sixty-five years of age. *Amer. J. Psychiat.* 102:168–73.

Clark, M., & Anderson, B. G. 1967. *Culture and aging*. Springfield: Charles C Thomas.

Cohen, Y. A. 1968. Culture as adaptation. In *Man in adaptation: The cultural present*. Chicago: Aldine.

Costner, H. L. 1965. Criteria for measures of association. *Amer. soc. Rev.* 30:341–53.

Cowgill, D. O. 1965. Social life of the aging in Thailand. Paper presented at annual meeting of the Gerontological Society, Los Angeles.

Elliott, H. W. 1886. *Our Arctic province: Alaska and the Seal Islands*. New York: Scribner's.

Elwin, V. 1947. *The Muria Gond and their ghotul*. Bombay: Oxford Univ. Press.

Goffman, E. 1959. *The presentation of self in everyday life*. Garden City: Doubleday Anchor.

————. 1963. *Stigma: Notes on the management of spoiled identity*. Englewood Cliffs: Prentice-Hall.

Hart, C. W. M., & Pilling, A. R. 1960. *The Tiwi of North Australia*. New York: Holt, Rinehart, & Winston.

Hediger, H. 1964. *Wild animals in captivity*. New York: Dover.

Holmberg, A. R. 1969. *Nomads of the long bow*. Garden City: Natural History Press.

Kalish, R. A. 1969. The effects of death upon the family. In *Death and dying*, ed. L. Pearson. Cleveland: Case Western Reserve Univ. Press.

Kastenbaum, R. 1964. The interpersonal context of death in a geriatric institution. Paper presented at annual meeting of the Gerontological Society, Minneapolis.

Koty, J. 1933. *Die Behandlung der Alten und Kranken bei den Naturvölkern*. Stuttgart: W. Kohlhammer.

Lee, R. B. 1969. Kung bushman subsistence: An input–output analysis. In *Environment and cultural behavior*, ed. A. P. Vayda. Garden City: Natural History Press.

————, & DeVore, I. 1968. *Man the hunter*. Chicago: Aldine.

Lieberman, M. 1961. The relationship of mortality rates to entrance to a home for the aged. *Geriatrics* 16:515–19.

Linton, R. 1942. Age and sex categories. *Amer. soc. Rev.* 7:589–603.

Maxwell, R. J. 1967. Onstage and offstage sex: Exploring an hypothesis. *Cornell J. soc. Rel.* 1:75–84.

————. 1970. The changing status of elders in a Polynesian society. *Aging and human development* 1:137–46.

Mead, M. 1956. *New lives for old: Cultural transformation—Manus 1928–1953*. New York: Wm. Morrow.

Menzel, H. 1953. A new coefficient for scalogram analysis. *Pub. Opin. Quart.* 17:268–80.

Murdock, G. P. 1968. World sampling provinces. *Ethnology* 7:305–26.

Nash, M. 1966. *Primitive and peasant economic systems*. San Francisco: Chandler.

Okada, Y. 1962a. Changing family relationships of older people in Japan during the last fifty years. In *Social and psychological aspects of aging*, ed. C. Tibbetts & W. Donahue. New York: Columbia Univ. Press.

————. 1962b. The aged in rural and urban Japan. In *Social and psychological aspects of aging*, ed. C. Tibbetts & W. Donahue. New York: Columbia Univ. Press.

Olson, R. L. 1930. *Chumash prehistory. Univ. Calif. Pub. in Amer. Arch. and Ethnol.* 28:1–21.

Riley, M. W., & Foner, A. 1968. *Aging and society: An inventory of research findings* vol. 1. New York: Russell Sage Foundation.

Roberts, J. M. 1951. *Three Navaho households: A comparative study in small group culture. Peabody Mus. Harvard Univ. Papers* 40, 3.

————. 1956. *Zuni daily life.* Univ. Neb. Lab. Anthro. Notebook no. 3, Monograph no. 2.

————. 1961. Zuni. In *Variations in value orientations,* ed. F. R. Kluckhohn & F. L. Strodtbeck. New York: Harper & Row.

————. 1964. The self-management of cultures. In *Explorations in cultural anthropology,* ed. W. Goodenough. New York: McGraw-Hill.

————, & Sutton-Smith, B. 1962. Child training and game involvement. *Ethnology* 1:166–85.

Rowe, W. L. 1961. The middle and later years in Indian society. In *Aging and leisure,* ed. R. W. Kleeimeir. New York: Oxford Univ. Press.

Sahlins, M. D., & Service, E. R. 1960. *Evolution and culture.* Ann Arbor: Univ. Mich. Press.

Shelton, A. J. 1969. Igbo child-rearing, eldership, and dependence: A comparison. In *The dependencies of old people,* ed. R. A. Kalish. Inst. Gerontol. Occasional Papers, no. 6, Univ. Mich.–Wayne State Univ.

Silverman, P. 1968. Local elites and the image of a nation: The incorporation of Barotseland within Zambia. Unpublished doctoral dissertation, Library, Cornell Univ., Ithaca.

Simmons, L. W. 1945. *The role of the aged in primitive society.* New Haven: Yale Univ. Press.

Spencer, P. 1965. *The Samburu: A study of gerontocracy in a nomadic tribe.* Berkeley: Univ. Calif. Press.

Valentine, C. A. 1961. *Masks and men in a Melanesian society.* Lawrence: Univ. Kan. Press.

White, L. A. 1949. *The science of culture.* New York: Grove Press.

————. 1959. *The evolution of culture.* New York: McGraw-Hill.

Whiting, J. W. M. 1964. Effects of climate on certain cultural practices. In *Explorations in cultural anthropology,* ed. W. Goodenough. New York: McGraw-Hill.

————. 1968. Methods and problems in cross-cultural research. In *The handbook of social psychology,* ed. G. Lindzey & E. Aronson, vol. 2, 2d ed. Reading: Addison-Wesley.

Young, F. W. 1965. *Initiation ceremonies: A cross-cultural study of status dramatization.* New York: Bobbs-Merrill.

chapter 2

TRENDS IN ANTHROPOLOGICAL GERONTOLOGY: FROM SIMMONS TO THE SEVENTIES

Lowell D. Holmes

This paper is concerned with anthropology's contribution to the study of aging, a subject matter area where each of us has the dubious privilege of doing participant observation. Although some of the studies which will be cited were actually carried out by other behavioral scientists, all of those discussed are "anthropological" in the sense that they are either:

1. cross cultural,
2. holistic in conception,
3. concerned with predictable patterns of traditional behavior, or
4. produced by researchers who identify as professional anthropologists.

What follows is a survey of the literature designed to introduce newcomers in gerontological research to anthropological perspectives and to serve as a review and critique for experienced hands. The focus is on three basic approaches which appear to have characterized anthropological research interests in the aged. They are:

1. status and role studies, relating particularly to economic and modernization factors,

35

2. self or societal conceptions and attitudes toward aging and old age, and
3. applied or pragmatic approaches which attempt to discover ways in which our society and our aged may better cope with the problems associated with advanced age.

Simmons' Pioneer Study of Role and Status

Anthropology's interest in the study of the aged began in 1945 with the publication of sociologist Leo Simmons' *The Role of the Aged in Primitive Society* [1]. An earlier encyclopedic volume by J. Koty called *Die Behandlung der Alten und Kranken bei den Naturvölkern* (1933) published in Stuttgart, apparently went unnoticed or at least unheralded in the United States.

Simmons' book directed attention at a segment of the population which heretofore had interested anthropologists only as sources of ethnographic information about earlier, and supposedly more traditional days. It represented "a report on the status and treatment of the aged within a world-wide selection of primitive societies," [2, p. 229] and did so by utilizing some rather elaborate and complicated statistical measurements. Indeed, it was described by one reviewer as "the first systematic comparative analysis of the role of the aged in primitive society" [3, 287].

Data taken from monographs on seventy-one widely distributed tribes were selected with an eye to differences in environment, level of technological development and degree of cultural complexity. Some 109 cultural traits pertaining to (1) habitat and economy, (2) religious beliefs and practices, and (3) social and political organization were correlated with 112 traits dealing particularly with factors of status and treatment of the aged. Included in this list were such variables as leadership at festivals, property rights, food sharing practices, community support, political authority and chieftainship.

While reviewers generally applauded the exhaustive methods in Simmons' pioneer effort they were not completely enthusiastic about the result. Hallowell questioned "whether or not the results obtained in this study justify the elaborate statistical means employed," and he added, "I do not think they do" [2]. He concluded, "I do not believe that this book will win any new adherents to quantitative ethnology." Kimball conceded that the work would "have value as a reference work" but criticized Simmons' methodology on the basis that "there is the ever-present danger that the use of isolated cultural facts, called 'traits,' outside their context may produce distortion of meaning" [3]. He also doubted "if culture lends itself to additive and statistical treatment except on the most limited level." More recently Robert Maxwell pronounced the Simmons study "of limited value, largely because of its flawed methodology" [4, p. 362]. He noted in particular the absence of careful sampling procedures, a lack of any statement of coding procedures, and errors in several statistical operations.

But what of the conclusions drawn from the Simmons research? While the study reported that status and treatment of the aged varied widely among the seventy-one groups there were also certain tendencies which appeared to be based in the level of technological development or in the complexity of the social organization. Generally, Simmons found that:

1. the status of the aged stemmed from the force of tradition and from the special skills and knowledge that they possessed,
2. that security for them was derived from property rights,
3. that food was assured through communal sharing, kinship obligations and from food tabus from which aged are exempt,
4. that their general welfare was at least in part the result of routine services of an economic and personal nature performed by the aged, and, finally,
5. that security derived from ability to wield civil and political power as a result of individual ability or as a combination of social and cultural conditions.

Generally it was found that obligations of kinsmen or special value of services to the family were the most important factors affecting the security of the aged.

The Simmons study is important because it suggested a direction which would be followed again and again by subsequent researchers. This is the role and status approach which attempts to correlate prestige and security with levels of subsistence or degrees of technological development.

Other Status and Role Studies

Irwin Press and Mike McKool have also investigated factors associated with high and low status for aged in a number of Middle American societies [5]. These researchers isolate four so-called "prestige generating" components operative in Meso-America and perhaps all societies. They are the *advisory,* the *contributory,* the *control,* and the *residual* components. The *advisory* component concerns the degree to which the advice and opinions of aged society members are heeded, whereas the *contributory* component has to do with the degree to which the aged participate in and contribute to ritual and economic activities. The *control* component pertains to the degree of direct authority the aged have over the behavior of other persons or institutions or ritual processes, and the *residual* component concerns the degree to which the aged retain prestige because of roles performed earlier in life. Press and McKool conclude that the aged are at a disadvantage where society is marked by features such as economic heterogeneity, diversity, and discontinuity in father-son economic interests. The status of the aged is also low where little importance is placed on ascriptive roles, where there is nuclear family independence and an early turnover of family resources, and where there is bureaucratization of ritual, political and judicial functions. While Press and McKool are not particularly interested in the dynamic aspects of the assignment of prestige, they tend to see the factors detracting from the prestige of the elderly as being highly associated with the process of "modernization."

Also approaching the subject of gerontology from a role and status perspective is the research of Robert J. Maxwell and Philip Silverman who utilize the "general rubric of system theory" [6, p. 363]. Maxwell and Silverman hypothesize that societies value their aged in varying degrees depending upon the amount of useful information they control. It is further assumed that this in turn is related to their social participation. An analysis of data from twenty-six widely distributed societies directed special attention to:

1. information control among the aged,
2. treatment of the aged,
3. rate of institutional change, and
4. ecological factors affecting the aged.

Analysis of the key variable—information control—was directed at participation in feasts and games, consulting, decision-making, entertaining, arbitrating, and teaching.

Maxwell and Silverman found a strong tendency for control of useful information to be associated with good treatment and high status among the aged, but they suggested that rapid institutional change, characteristic of industrialized societies, generates a high rate of information obsolescence and thus leads to an apparent deterioration of prestige for the aged.

The impact of cultural change on the fortunes and activities of the aged also represented a central focus in the study by Donald O. Cowgill and Lowell D. Holmes [7]. Modernization, equated here with industrialization, urbanization and Westernization, was studied as a major factor affecting the elderly in fourteen societies ranging from what traditionally have been called "primitive" to those of Western Europe and the United States. The study differed from those of Simmons and Maxwell and Silverman in that aging was considered in terms of the complete cultural context.

The contributors to this study—eight anthropologists, seven sociologists, two psychologists and a social worker—had all carried out extended, in-depth studies in the societies on which they reported. Each was given a list of topics which provided some uniformity and continuity to the several studies but the contributors were ignorant of the general theoretical propositions that Cowgill and Holmes were testing. The theoretical orientation for the study consisted of a number of propositions predicting how the aged would be affected as one advanced on a societal continuum from primitive to modern society. Of the thirty propositions, eight were labelled universals and twenty-two were identified as "variations" (to be considered in terms of unique social and cultural contexts). The uniqueness of the contexts were in this case related to the society's position on the primitive-modern continuum.

The several studies, written without knowledge of the general theory, tend to support the initial propositions that generally hold that status decreases with modernization, but there were notable exceptions. Places such as Israel, Russia and Ireland extend higher status to the aged than would normally be expected from modern industrial nations, but some of these contradictions may be attributed to particular historical developments. This was not unanticipated by the investigators, however, and Holmes contends that, "How a society develops and changes under the impact of modernizing forces depends to a great extent upon the values it held previously. A society whose major religion is Buddhism may be quite differently affected by industrialization and urbanization than one operating under a Judeo-Christian tradition. The same is true for traditional differences in political or economic philosophy" [7, p. 87] .

Societal Attitudes Toward Aging

Turning now to self or societal conceptions of aging, we note the study of attitudes toward old age elicited from 5,500 men aged eighteen—thirty-two by V. L. Bengston and D. H. Smith [8] . Four hour interviews were conducted with respondents from Argentina, Chile, India, Pakistan, Israel and Nigeria. Hypothesizing that being aged would be more negatively regarded in modern, industrialized societies as compared with traditional social settings, the investigators specifically tested the following hypotheses:

1. perception of the instrumental value of old people is inversely related to the degree of modernity exhibited by individuals,
2. positive attitudes toward one's own aging are inversely related to modernity, and
3. obligations toward, and prerequisites of, the aged are inversely related to modernity.

Evidence failed to support any of these hypotheses. In fact, there was evidence of a direct rather than an inverse relationship between modernity and positive attitudes toward aging. Individual and social modernity had little systematic influence on attitudes toward aging. It was further discovered that status accorded to the aged is not substantially higher in more traditional as compared with more modern settings.

A further exploration into societal attitudes toward growing old has been reported by Robert J. Smith, Allan Holmberg, Charles Hughes and others [9] . Anthropologists familiar with the cultures of Quechua Indians, Greenland Eskimos, Japanese, Burmese and the people of northern India assessed the relationship between negative or positive conceptions of aging with concepts of time in these various societies. The question is posed, for example, as to whether or not the accurate measurement of time places a special accent on the passing years and is responsible for a less favorable attitude toward aging than is to be found in societies with simpler technology where time is less emphasized. It is suggested that a society that tells people at birth how many years they can expect to live and tells them precisely the date on which they will be required to relinquish their place in the labor force cannot help but generate anxiety, particularly when it then proceeds to have Western Union monitored time machines accurately and obviously tick away the hours, days and years. Such anxiety, of course, depends a great deal upon the value placed on life and purposeful labor, but world-wide surveys of attitudes toward longevity conducted by other researchers [7] tend to indicate that most old people the world over want to live as long as possible provided they are healthy and comfortable, and that they value opportunities to contribute to their society's operation as long as they are able. In many societies age is not calculated in years at all but in terms of ability to perform tasks, either physical or mental [9]. Many societies, furthermore, place emphasis on increased wisdom and experience gained through living a long time rather than on the decreasing number of years remaining until death or retirement. Where time is not kept accurately there is the further possibility of a more gradual transition from an active to less active life and consequently a greater ability to come to terms with the phenomenon of declining strength and vigor.

Margaret Clark and Barbara Anderson reported the results of research among 435 San Francisco aged [10]. Comprising the sample were 284 "normal" people from the community who were sixty years of age and older, eighty-one inpatients of the psychiatric ward, and ninety former patients of that ward at San Francisco General Hospital who were then living at home. Basic variables studied were self evaluation, morale, status index, and level of social interaction. Besides establishing a precedent for anthropologists using traditional anthropological methods in studying the aged in their own society, this study contributed to a growing fund of information concerning the dilemma or crisis of growing old in America. Maintaining that the major threats to the well-being of the aged consist of weak kinship ties, rapid technological change, relative and absolute increases in the number of aged, and in the sacred cows of American culture—independence and productivity—Clark and Anderson suggest avenues of survival which might, in opposition to disengagement theory, be labelled "relaxation." If aging Americans are to achieve positive self-image and morale, adjustment must come in their:

1. acceptance of physical and mental change,
2. willingness to relinquish certain roles and activities,
3. ability to substitute alternative sources of need gratification,
4. modification of their basis for self-judgment and,
5. in general, their ability to find a new place in the larger scheme of things.

Truly an anthropological study of aging, the work of Clark and Anderson utilizes culture not as a back-drop but rather as a configuration of active principles in a complex psycho-cultural matrix.

Equally concerned with culture as a dynamic force in aging perceptions was Austin Shelton, whose 1965 study of mental and emotional stability among the Nsukka Ibo aged reports a "virtual absence of psycho-senility or even a sense of indolence or disengagement" in that eastern Nigerian society [11]. Shelton suggests that psycho-senility has generally been considered as resulting almost solely from physiological deterioration associated with advanced age, but that it should more profitably be re-examined in terms of the characteristics of the cultural milieu.

In Ibo society Shelton finds a very positive attitude toward growing old, coupled with a decline in stress situations. The aged have an important role in the religious life because they supposedly enjoy the good will of the ancestors, and have a strong economic position with support guaranteed by both family and clan. They are past the time when they must face the problems of procuring lands, wives and titles. Vanished also is the anxiety over being able to father or bear a son and such tribulations as antagonistic spirits or the necessity of leaving the village to seek employment are removed. Shelton thus argues against the inevitability of psycho-senility and suggests that among Ibo elders the ability to perform useful tasks and command respect are more commonly a matter of culture than biology.

The aged in Iboland have actually had more than their share of attention by anthropologists. In addition to Shelton, Malcolm Arth has also devoted considerable time to gerontological studies. Shelton and Arth, however, differ considerably in conceptualization and interpretation of Ibo values and behavior. Arth questions Shelton's claims of a placid old age for Ibo, maintaining that today there is considerable ambivalence of attitude toward the aged [12]. Acculturation has tended to increase stresses and differences in values between generations, as evidenced by frequent outbursts and conflicts between the young and the old. There is an underlying hostility toward the aged, perhaps because they are reminders of mortality. Arth also questions Shelton's definition of "psycho-senility." Drawing upon data from a study of psychiatric disorders, not among the Ibo but among the Yoruba, Arth reports that "senility is not considered abnormal, and that such patients would usually not be hospitalized" [13, p. 243]. Could it be, asks Arth, that "Shelton's informants were speaking about cultural ideals" whereas Arth's research tended to focus on the behavioral level?

Stereotypes concerning old age were the topic of a cross-cultural study by Arnhoff, Leon and Lorge [14]. As a test of the universality of what has been purported to be "negative beliefs or stereotypes" which are accepted in this country, the researchers compared questionnaire responses from sample populations of 300 each in five countries—Great Britain, Sweden, Greece, Japan and Puerto Rico. The investigators were "struck by the overall ubiquitousness of the beliefs, transcending geography, education and cultural differences." Perceptions of old age appeared to be predominantly negative everywhere, regardless of culture [14, p. 56].

Pragmatic Approaches

In the area of applied or pragmatic approaches to the problems of aging Margaret Mead has been the major spokesman, although Jules Henry and Margaret Clark have contributed significantly [15, 16]. A quarter of a century ago, Mead suggested reducing the social and experiential distance between generations by the creation of GPTA's (Grandparent-Teacher Associations), making occupational shifts in middle life which offer some measure of recognition for later life, and getting involved with younger people outside the family by switching to younger medical practitioners, lawyers, bankers, stock brokers, etc. [17]. More recently, Mead has suggested that it has not been the young who have "copped out" on their responsibilities to society, but rather the old [18]. By withdrawing they have deprived the young of a model of what it is to age, to be old and to die. Grandparents of today, Mead maintains, have seen more change during their lifetime than any generation that has ever lived, and they therefore have special knowledge which should be made available to younger generations. For example, they need to reassure the young that change does not mean the end of the world but only the end of a particular kind of world. A notoriously useful grandmother herself, Mead insists that there are myriad ways in which the aged can contribute, but that they will first have to give up the martyrdom of old age that she believes some find satisfying.

Margaret Clark feels that anthropologists can contribute to the solution of our aged's problems by gaining a better understanding of those societies where the values which are forced upon our aged are already the core values of the culture. Such a society would be one which features what George Foster has labelled the "Image of the Limited Good" [19]. Where this values exists, any deliberate striving for goods or prestige is seen as evil, as it is believed that such commodities are in short supply, and to actively seek them is to attempt to deprive others. In Clark's opinion, if our aged are to remain mentally healthy they must be educated to accept the concept of "limited good" and relinquish the Cinderella myth, the Colonel Sanders' fable and the Protestant Ethic.

Suggestions for Further Research

A number of gerontological topics remain to be explored. Anthropologists with their holistic, functional approach may be the most qualified of social scientists to do the job. Among the more challenging is the concept of a double standard of aging, a phenomenon found in our society and perhaps in others. The fact that cultural ideas prescribe that aging is more permissible in men than women and that the former remain eligible for marriage longer in spite of their shorter life span has a profound effect on personality development, interpersonal relations and social structure.

Equally in need of study is the matter of personality development into later life. Personality continues to change as life experiences change but this dynamic process has been little documented. David Gutmann, a psychologist with cross-cultural interests, utilized TAT data from two cultures—Mayan and North American—in a study of changing ego states, i.e., perceptions of self and the world [20]. In a Kansas City sample of 140 men aged forty to seventy Gutmann identified men forty—fifty-four as exhibiting an ego state labelled *active mastery* which involved a pursuit of achievement and independence and an attempt to control external conditions. Men fifty-five—sixty-four exhibited traits of *passive mastery*, which involved more internal control than external and a great tendency to accommodate. Those sixty-five and over exhibited *magical mastery* tendencies wherein self-deception and denial of unpleasant reality became characteristic. Gutmann believes that he found many similarities between his Kansas City sample and sixty-three Mayan corn farmers in Yucatan. The only striking difference noted was a greater sense of guilt and remorse for earlier aggressive pursuits among the aged in the North American sample. A number of methodological weaknesses are apparent in this study but investigations of this type will hopefully continue in spite of the problems involved in crossing cultural boundaries [21].

Kiefer suggests a number of topics relating to social stratification that deserve the attention of anthropologists interested in aging [22]. Questions of the extent to which acculturation and marginality affect the lives of the minority aged remain to be answered as well as questions dealing with differential attitudes and behavior regarding disengagement, self-reliance, dependency and anxiety among representatives of different social classes.

Further studies into the relationship between culture and biology (such as those giving rise to the Ibo senility debate or ones which would give explanations for the claimed extreme longevity among some Russian and Greek populations) should be undertaken, as should studies of demography and political organization. The fact that the aged in America represent an increasingly larger percentage of the population and that they have one of the best voting records makes this a segment of the population with great political potential. Perhaps anthropologists should reacquaint themselves with the world's forms of gerontocracies in preparation for dealing with our own political future.

Whatever the subject of study it must be realized that the aged are no longer viewed by anthropologists as just the storehouses of tradition as Boasian field-workers conceived them, and that the study of the life cycle is incomplete without documentation of the latter years.

REFERENCES

1. L. Simmons, *The Role of the Aged in Primitive Society*. Yale University Press, New Haven, 1945.
2. A. Hallowell, Review of Leo Simmons' *The Role of the Aged in Primitive Society*. *Annals of the American Academy, 244*, p. 229, 1946.
3. T. Kimball, Review of Leo Simmons' *The Role of the Aged in Primitive Society*. *American Journal of Sociology, 52*, p. 287, 1946.
4. R. J. Maxwell, The Changing Status of Elders in a Polynesian Society. *Aging and Human Development, 1*, pp. 137-146, 1970.

5. I. Press and M. McKool, Social Structure and Status of the Aged: Toward Some Valid Cross-cultural Generalizations. *Aging and Human Development, 3*, pp. 297-306, 1972.
6. R. J. Maxwell and P. Silverman, Information and Esteem: Cultural Considerations in the Treatment of the Aged. *Aging and Human Development, 1*:4, pp. 361-392, 1970.
7. D. Cowgill and L. D. Holmes, *Aging and Modernization,* Appleton, Century, Crofts, New York, 1972.
8. V. L. Bengtson and D. H. Smith, Social Modernity and Attitudes Toward Aging. *The Gerontologist, 8* (3, pt. 2), p. 26 (abstract), 1968.
9. R. Smith, R. Holmberg and C. Hughes et al., Cultural Differences and the Concept of Time. *Aging and Leisure,* R. W. Kleemeier (ed.), Oxford University Press, New York, 1961.
10. M. Clark and B. Anderson, *Culture and Aging,* Charles Thomas, Springfield, 1967.
11. A. J. Shelton, Ibo Aging and Eldership: Notes for Gerontologists and Others. *The Gerontologist, 5,* pp. 20-23, 1965.
12. M. J. Arth, An Interdisciplinary View of the Aged in Ibo Culture. *Journal of Geriatric Psychiatry, 2,* pp. 33-39, 1968.
13. M. J. Arth, Ideals and Behavior. A Comment on Ibo Respect Patterns. *The Gerontologist, 8,* pp. 242-244, 1968.
14. F. N. Arnhoff, H. V. Leone and I. Lorge, Cross-cultural Acceptance of Stereotypes Toward Aging. *Journal of Social Psychology, 63,* pp. 41-58, 1964.
15. J. Henry, *Culture Against Man,* Random House, New York, 1963.
16. M. Clark, Contributions of Cultural Anthropology to the Study of the Aged. *Cultural Illness and Health,* L. Nader and T. W. Maretzki (eds.), American Anthropological Association (Anthropological Studies, No. 9), Washington, D.C., 1973.
17. M. Mead, Cultural Contexts of Aging. *No Time to Grow Old,* Legislative Committee on the Problems of Aging Legislature Document No. 12, Albany, New York, 1951.
18. M. Mead, A New Style of Aging. *Christianity and Crisis, 31:*19, pp. 240-243, 1971.
19. G. Foster, Peasant Society and the Image of Limited Good. *American Anthropologist, 67,* pp. 293-315, 1965.
20. D. L. Gutmann, An Exploration of Ego Configurations in Middle and Late Life. *Personality in Middle and Late Life,* B. L. Neugarten et al. (eds.), Atherton Press, New York, 1964.
21. I. Press, Maya Aging: Cross-cultural Projective Techniques and the Dilemma of Interpretation, *Psychiatry, 30,* pp. 197-202, 1967.
22. C. W. Kiefer, Notes on Anthropology and the Minority Elderly. *The Gerontologist, 11* (pt. 2), pp. 94-98, 1971.

part two

RELATIVE AGE: LOOKING AROUND THE WORLD

chapter 3

SOCIAL STRUCTURE AND STATUS OF THE AGED: TOWARD SOME VALID CROSS-CULTURAL GENERALIZATIONS

Irwin Press and Mike McKool Jr.

Aging, like the proverbial elephant, has been partially defined by many, yet still remains an incompletely known phenomenon. To describe the process in terms of accumulated intra-nerve cell deposition of the pigment lipofuscin, or in terms of a host of other specific accumulating physical-chemical changes is to describe somewhat the condition of the vessel (e.g., Lansing 1959). The "cargo," however, is quite another matter.

The relationship between physiological and psychosocial expressions of aging is still unclear. Much that we had thought were "automatic" ego-state shifts through the maturation process might be more dependent upon cultural than physiological variables. Shelton, for example, has noted that Ibo males (Nigeria) exhibit no "psycho senility" or "disengagement" as they age (1965:20). He attributes this absence to specific cultural phenomena such as high ritual, arbitrational and advisory status accorded old men. Much of our knowledge about aging is based upon observation and inference from western industrial society. Some supposedly general processes (regression, disengagement, etc.) may be strictly limited to this milieu. There is, of course, no reason why certain processes or determinants of status derived from western societies may not be validly representative of universal phenomena. Yet as Shanas notes, it is unlikely that "a hypothesis about social behavior [can] be considered proved by a study carried out within a single culture . . ." (1963:7). Similar doubts have been voiced by Cowgill (1971), Burgess (1960:386) and others. Both Shanas and Burgess, however, find the comparative mandate satisfied by cross-national (rather than cross-cultural) studies within the Western industrialized community.

Unfortunately, it cannot be said that our present knowledge of *non*-Western societies facilitates the development of validly universal generalizations or hypotheses about aging. Simmons' lament of 1945 is still largely apropos. "Ethnographers," he claimed, "have been none too careful in reporting all relevant information on the status and treatment of the aged, or in placing it in convenient categories" (1945:19).[1] Simmons' own ground-breaking examination of cultural, social and ecological determinants of status of the aged in some seventy-one primitive societies reflected this weakness. By and large, he correlated a hodge podge of variables resulting in many interesting hypothetical points and an overall lack of coherence. Missing is a feeling for the interplay of factors which, in any given society, combine in specified ways to determine status of the aging individual. For example, Simmons' statistical correlations indicate that high status goes with patrilineal, patrilocal descent-residence patterns. At the same time, prestige of the aged is higher in sedentary horticultural societies than in mobile or foraging societies. In that most matrilineal societies are horticultural and minimally mobile, one would thus wish to know more about the specific relationship between mobility and descent insofar as both affect status of the aged in any particular society. A scatter-gun approach fails to resolve the contradiction. Notwithstanding this weakness, Simmons succeeded in calling attention to a host of socio-cultural phenomena—some more obvious, some less obvious—which may affect both status of the aged (in terms of role opportunities) and perception and treatment of them (prestige indicators).

More recently, Cowgill has attempted to pull together a number of "scattered, disparate sources" for the purpose of postulating a limited number of ostensibly universal generalizations about status of the aged (1971). Cowgill sees status of the aged as higher where: 1. accumulation of knowledge is important; 2. the aged can maintain property rights; 3. the aged may continue to perform useful functions; 4. the aged operate within an extended family structure; 5. there are fewer role shifts through maturation and thus, where the aged are less likely to become obsolete; and 6. there is less emphasis upon individual ego development.

Cowgill's determinants of status, it will be noticed, exhibit an overall consistency. Status of the aged, furthermore, is tied directly to the interactional or power-controlling aspects of roles occupied, rather than to such general—and less readily comparable—structural or cultural principles as "matriliny" or "sedentarism." All structural principles find expression through social statuses. Social statuses in turn can be at least partially described in terms of the power, influence or differentiation from others of their role incumbents. It is thus suggested that Cowgill's determinants are highly generalizable and may indeed have universal validity. These determinants were inductively derived piecemeal from a number of societies, thus their ultimate validity hangs upon their ability to explain status of the aged within any specific society or societal type.

This first test, as a matter of fact, has already been made. Coincidentally, at the same meeting in which Cowgill presented these hypotheses, the present authors introduced the

---

[1] By way of example, Reina notes that old age is defined in Chinaulta (Guatemala) as that time "when a person is physically unable to carry on the most basic tasks in maintaining the operation of a household." These tasks are left undefined, however. He goes on to state that "when a person begins to feel his strength ebbing away, he feels that he has indeed reached old age, that he will soon die and that he is no longer of any use to anyone. At this precise moment, the respect the man is used to and enjoys begins to decrease rapidly, as his former status and role in the pueblo vanish." (1966:252) It is unlikely that any such "moment" (short of instantaneous invalidity from stroke, etc.) comes with "precision." Nor are the phenomena surrounding this moment detailed for us. Raymond Firth, too, notes that as a Tikopian ages, the children "take upon themselves more of the responsibility of the family affairs," of "directing the family policy" and of participating in the family conclave. However, in the same cryptic half paragraph, Firth repeats three times that younger members "defer" to the aging male's opinion (1965:165), thus leaving us once more in the dark as to the *de facto* "status" of the aged in Tikopia.

results of a preliminary analysis of aging in Meso-American peasant society (Press and McKool, 1971). We, too, attempted to derive general determinants of status of the aged. *Almost point for point, our independently derived determinants coincided with Cowgill's.* Though originally we had given no thought to generalizing beyond aging in peasant societies, we now believe that our determinants have general validity. Before commenting further on their nature, it is necessary to illustrate the kinds of data from which they were derived or, from the point of view of Cowgill's hypotheses, the kinds of real situations to which they can apply. Accordingly, the major elements of the Meso-American peasant analysis are summarized below. Both Cowgill's and our own "structural determinants" are represented here. Where his offer a somewhat different orientation, they are included in parentheses.

STATUS OF AGED PEASANTS IN MEXICO AND GUATEMALA

Though differing in a number of ways, most peasant communities of Mexico and Guatemala exhibit certain similar characteristics. Farming is the major source of income. Most farmers consume at least a part of their produce. Corn is the staple. Technology is largely pre-Colombian, generally involving digging stick and, often, slash and burn techniques. Nominally Catholic, the people celebrate an annual round of individual saints days and village patron saint rituals. Priests are of minimal importance, ritual content and direction falling to villagers themselves. Considerable funds may be expended in such ritual. Secular display is generally frowned upon and may be minimized through institutionalized witchcraft fears. Communities are small and close knit to the extent that marriages are generally endogamous with respect to the village and that residents closely identify themselves with their towns. Inter-community mobility (permanent moving) is minimal.

Young men and women take up adult economic tasks at an early age. Role choices tend to be minimal and males are frequently forced into participation in civil and/or ritual institutions. There are few specialty roles beyond that of curer. Where potting, weaving or other skills can bring in good income, most in the community engage in them, thus once again limiting the number of specialty roles and avenues for unusual achievement.

The structural determinants

1. The more socio-economically homogeneous the community, the higher the status of the aged. Concomitantly, the fewer the alternatives available in life-cycle roles, the higher the status. (Where there is less emphasis upon individual ego development, the higher the status.)

The homogeneity factor in itself does not logically create higher status or prestige for the aged, for if all are viewed alike, why will the older be differentiated from the youthful family head or child? "Homogeneity" refers, rather, to minimal role differentiation at each stage of life, and minimal difference between the life-cycle role sequences or stages which each individual passes through. Logically, therefore, differentiation can arise through the simple accumulation of universally available roles: the more roles, the older.

Even where active high power roles cease with a certain level of physical disability, the individual is already differentiated from those who have yet to complete an active role-life. The old person may continue to be accorded at least the same prestige he had when last active.

The existence of significant economic alternatives in a community may readily lead to differential success and access to scarce commodities (both physical and social). Age may cease to be the *sine qua non* of resource control and expertise where fathers and sons engage in different activities with differing degrees of success. Economic independence of the children may lead to decreased importance of elder-dominated extended family households. Wealth differentials, in the more closed peasant community, may lead, furthermore, to an increase in witchcraft and envy and thus, as in Tzo'ontahal, Chiapas, discourage performance in traditionally visible conspicuous consumption positions usually dominated by elders (June Nash 1970:279. See Eric Wolf, 1957, for an enlightening discussion of the homogeneity requirements of "closed, corporate peasant communities").

In Chinautla, the growing needs of nearby Guatemala City are encouraging new economic activities, whereby younger men may earn considerably more than did or do their fathers from corn and charcoal production (Reina 1966: chapter 4). Old men in Chinautla are a burden upon the young and often resented. "There is little respect for the old," Reina concludes (p. 252-3). Manning Nash has noted similar changes in another Guatemalan town, Cantel, where the advent of a factory has offered unprecedented economic alternatives to young men and women. Aging parents are dependent upon their children, regardless of whether the children engage in agriculture or factory wage labor. The parents of factory workers, however, are generally supported in the children's home, and this "reverses former dependency relations and violates cultural expectations. It is different from the agricultural instances, which usually result from the father giving the son the house and land upon which the father will later be supported . . ." Nash goes on to point out that while parents "are given the respect and deference due them because of their kinship category . . . they are stripped of authority and power by the circumstance of being under a roof kept by others." (Nash, 1969, 71). Here a "residual" status is compartmentalized from a direct control or power status. One cannot help but wonder whether even residual prestige in Cantel is not destined for erosion.

Where sequential life roles are largely ascribed, differential prestige, as noted above, may arise through the simple accumulation of available roles and skills. Using TATs in a Yucatan peasant community, Gutmann (1966) has claimed to find a decrease in generalized guilt among aging peasant males. Press (1967), working in the same community, suggests that this is due, above all, to the lack of alternative roles through the life cycle. Traditionally, there has been no alternative to dressing as a mestizo (shoeless), speaking Maya, marrying locally, residing patrilocally upon marriage, farming corn and teaching one's sons to farm corn. The simple accumulation of these entails progressively higher prestige, and the final dependence upon one's sons is felt to be deserved.

Finally, it is likely that where ascriptive village-service roles are common, a certain automatic level of prestige accrues to any man who has "done his duty." Foster notes that "in Tzintzuntzan and in other peasant societies, the conspicuous consumption that underlies the mayordomia system leads to prestige, not because it calls attention to productive or acquisitive capacity, but because, in a different way, it permits a man to show visibly that he conforms to the ideal type of his society. It permits him to emphasize his commitment to the equality principle which means a healthy community. He, more than anyone else, is equal, and because of his dedication to the ideal that is seen as spelling social stability, his society not only can afford to extend to him prestige, but it must do so (Foster 1967:208).

2. Where sequential roles entail progressively higher responsibility, authority or advisory capacity, the higher the status of the aged. From yet another point of view, (where the accumulation of knowledge is experiential and thus subject to increment with age, the higher the status of older individuals).

We are describing an automatic increment, where by default, older men occupy higher statuses than younger who are still "on the way up." In many communities, ritual office holders must rely heavily upon the step-by-step guidance of older ex-officials (often called "principales"). These men are highly respected and may, furthermore, control appointment of the office holders themselves.

The civil-religious or *cargo* system of Meso-America is perhaps a classic example of an ascriptive role sequence producing control by the more mature. In communities such as Mitla (Parsons 1936:164), all or most men actually pass through the sequence. June Nash describes a Chiapan town where, depending upon economic resources, the average man will not complete his obligation until he is from fifty to sixty-five years old (1970:172). In other communities, such as Cheran (Beals 1946), or Yalalag (de la Fuente 1949:214) highest positions are effectively limited to men who have accumulated friends, contacts, reciprocal (*compadre*) bonds and economic resources sufficient to discharge the demanding obligations. Such men will generally, though not invariably, be more mature. Now, we are not suggesting that a "halo effect" automatically will extend higher prestige to all older men because the few positions of highest prestige are occupied by some older men. It is simply more likely than would be the case if the more important positions were regularly occupied by the younger.

3. Where the life style role sequence can be described in terms of "continuity," the higher will be the status of the aged. Furthermore, the fewer the number of role shifts in the life cycle, the less likely the older will become obsolete.

Essentially, this reflects Benedict's earlier distinction between continuity and discontinuity in preparation for sequential roles (1938). It is here suggested that where role transitions are gradual or minimally traumatic, with ample preparation, there will be less overt or conceptual stages in the life cycle. In short, the distinction between older and younger individuals will be less clear-cut. Press has described how in the Yucatec Maya peasant community, the individual's departure from corn farming and other activities is as gradual and imperceptible as his entry into them. Thus there is no clear point at which the aging male becomes a "has been" (1967). Peasant farming or simple craft economic systems are particularly apt to entail such graduality of role passage, though early turnover of property to children can mitigate later prestige.

4. Where control of important family or community resources or processes are in the hands of the older members, the higher will be the status of the aged.

This would be particularly the case where, again, highest cargo positions are reserved for older individuals, or where organization of certain important ritual activity is a perquisite of age. Wolf notes that in Meso-America in general, control of ritual tends to be in the hands of older community members. Through control of ritual resources, the old gain "moral ascendency" and thus power over others (1959:215-223). J. Nash describes how older community members have traditionally controlled knowledge of the power and desires of ancestral spirits. Today, however, as belief in the ancestors and their agents (the curers) wanes, roles of traditional importance for mature encumbents (such as *principal* and *alferex*) are vastly weakened and their function minimal. Indeed, today, to be a *principal* in Tzo'ontahal is to be a "has-been." It has become more a position of shame than prestige (J. Nash 1970:195). The growth of cooperatives and other economic innovations in Nash's town has allowed an increase in wealth differentials which thwart traditional leveling mechanisms such as envy and heavy ritual expenses. Successful, mature villagers fear those highly visible conspicuous-expenditure positions which now attract far more witchcraft accusations—and homicide attempts—than formerly. In Tepoztlan, too, Lewis equates loss of prestige among older men with loss of control over political-ritual positions and traditional lore.

In terms of family, rather than community resource control, Villa Rojas (1946) and Guiteras Holmes (1961) have both observed that breakdown of elder-controlled communal land holdings leads to break-up of extended family residence patterns. In Chinautla, "land has generally been under the management of the extended family. However, the present trend, which is not unique to Chinautla, is toward more individually owned property" (Reina 1966:43). Today in Chinautla, bitter and lasting disputes over property inheritance split brothers from one another and fathers from sons. As we noted earlier, old men receive low prestige in the town. Similar property disputes are reported from Tzo'ontahal, where prestige of the aged is also waning. It is of course possible for oldsters to acquire a new status to replace an eroding one. Reina notes that knowledge of curing techniques in Chinautla, notwithstanding loss of economic control, may preserve "an older person's good social standing" (1966:34).

A most suggestive example of family resource control is provided by Laura Nader's comparison of two Zapotec communities. In Juquila, "a son does not usually inherit his share of land officially until the death of his parents . . . . He continues to work the land in common with his father and brothers as long as the father lives." Fathers and sons live in the same house or close to one another. The son remains legally propertyless until the old man's death, and the extended family remains strong with the old man as leader and property controller. In the town of Talea, on the other hand, a son generally "receives his share of land legally at the time of marriage, and from that time on, he is responsible for working his own land, independently of his father, and apart from his father's household." The father sheds all economic responsibility for the son at his marriage. Nader notes that in Juquila, the nuclear family remains functioning "as a unit while its sons are acquiring their own families of procreation. In Talea, inheritance at marriage serves to separate a son from his family of orientation when he embarks upon his own family of procreation . . . Thus the Juquilan continues to function as a unit . . . whereas the Talean family experiences discontinuity" (1964:246). Nader concludes that paternal authority—and ostensibly prestige—is stronger where fathers maintain jural control over scarce resources longer, and where they live close by those over whom they ostensibly have authority (p. 289). June Nash, too, notes that the Tzo'ontahal father is expected to divide and surrender his property to his sons by the time he reaches age sixty-five. Delay has actually led to patricide (pp. 113, 279).

5. Where the old may engage in valued (and useful) activities longer, the higher will be their status.

Certain behaviors may be "useful," though not highly valued. It is doubtful whether baby-sitting—an activity generally associated with women—regularly confers meaningful prestige upon an old male. The definition of "engage in," is also relative. Simple supervison of agricultural work may constitute sufficient participation to identify a man as "actively engaged." Similarly, a switch from active production of food to at-home processing of foodstuffs (shelling, sorting, curing, etc.) may maintain the oldster in an "active" status.

It would seem that in craft communities, particularly, old people would be able to carry out direct activities longer than in agricultural (or, of course, hunting societies). In Tonala, for example, old potters are quite common. Even minimally ambulatory men may continue to supervise the work of sons in or near the house. Lewis describes a different situation in Tepoztlan, however. "It is not old age as such that is feared by the Tepoztecans, but dependence on others, or the inability to be self supporting. Most old people work until they can no longer stand . . . . There are few non-strenuous jobs for old men who can no longer farm. The lack of handicraft skills or other means of support is a real handicap to these men" (1960:83).

6. Where the extended family is a viable residential or economic unit, the higher will be the status of the aged.

We are referring to households in which the younger remain or return to live with the elder. This contrasts with situations wherein the elder has come to reside as dependent and "guest." In the extended family residential unit, the old maintain unbroken membership and duties in a viable social group. There is no clear break in the elder's dominant status, particularly where there is no clear turn-over of property or other right prior to the elder's death. In most instances, the aging individual retains titular ownership of the house itself.

Romney describes the authority which Mixtecan grandparents have over grandchildren and daughters-in-law in the patrilocal extended family (1966:117). This authority has been noted by Diaz among extended family households in Tonala (1966:74-75). On the other hand, in Chinautla loss of extended family viability goes hand in hand with low, dependent status of the aged. Perhaps more subtly and importantly, residence within the family entails continuity of responsibilities which, though simple, maintain the maturing individual in "active" rather than totally passive roles.

Where the economic unit is largely coterminous with the extended family, the elder members *de facto* remain economically active and may exert considerable control over the behavior of others. In Tonala, 53 percent of the families are engaged in potting, and the oldest male retains the position of head potter as long as he can use his hands. His influence over instruction, sales and pot design may last longer than his ability to actively work.

In many Meso-American communities, furthermore, initial virilocal residence generally means that a maturing male has housed and acted as household head to a succession of married sons and is often still the provider of shelter to the youngest at the time of his death. Thus, the question of whether the old parents are unwelcome dependents or generous providers remains ambiguous, and the oldster's status need not decline. This is particularly likely to be the case where village land is limited in area and privately owned, and where ejidal status of surrounding lands prevents construction of new, private homesteads.

STATUS GENERATES PRESTIGE

These structural determinants reflect many common elements of Meso-American peasant life, while accommodating internal variations as well. They are nonetheless general enough to subsume wide varieties of specific social, economic, ritual and political behavior in other cultural milieux.

Each of these structural determinants can be viewed as describing a continuum. Homogeneity may range from high to low, as can participation in "valued and useful" activities, etc. Societies, furthermore, may differ widely in degree to which each determinant varies with or complements others. To merely state that the society is "simple" or more "folk like" is not to be able to predict precisely which—if any—determinant will offer the aged a position of prestige. Thus in peasant craft communities, the possibility of continued economic function may offer high (or at least undiminished) prestige to the aged. Among certain Australian aborigine groups, on the other hand, active economic participation may give way to ritual control by elders over such important resourses as water holes. Yet among certain Eskimo groups, there was little recourse but death for elders who could no longer actively participate in the hunt or household activity.

"Status" and "prestige" have often been used synonymously in reference to the aged. Prestige is better viewed as a function of status. It is evidenced through the manner in which others interact with the aged person. Prestige may be exhibited through a host of behaviors, including deference, obedience, gesture, serving and seating arrangements, terms of address, advice-asking and other mechanisms which reflect inequality between the aged and the more youthful.

Status generates prestige. With reference to the aged, it is suggested that the prestige generating components of status are limited in number. The six structural determinants of status may, in fact, be reduced economically to four basic prestige generating components. These are:

1. *an advisory component,* reflected in the degree to which the advice or opinion of the aged individual is actually heeded. This results from expertise which the oldster has acquired through earlier experience and which is still useful to others. It does *not* describe situations wherein the aged are asked their advice simply because it is expected or would prevent slight or embarrassment.

2. *a contributory component,* reflected in the extent to which older society members

may still actively participate in traditional ritual, domestic or economic activities and make valued contributions to them.

3. *a control component*, reflecting the degree of direct control which the aged individual may exert over the behavior or welfare of others, through monopoly over necessary objects, property, ritual processes or knowledge.

4. *a residual component*, reflecting the degree to which aged individuals are associated with previous statuses no longer held, and thus accorded prestige in the absence of other, active components. It is likely that prestige largely based upon this component is more likely to co-exist with mixed feelings—and perhaps guilt—on the part of both the aged and others.

Each of these components is sufficient to generate prestige for the aged. While it is tempting to say "the more components operating, the higher the prestige," there is no evidence for its necessity. Rather, it is sufficient to say that the more in operation, the more likely that older individuals in the society will be accorded prestige. Referring back, once again, to our six structural determinants, this is to suggest that prestige of the aged will decline with increase in:

(a) societal economic heterogeneity; (b) diversity and discontinuity of father-son economic interests; (c) roles offering control or influence to the young;[2] (d) minimization of number and importance of ascriptive roles in general; (e) nuclear family independence; (f) non-household economic activity; (g) early turnover of family resources; and (h) bureaucratization of ritual, political and juridicial functions (though this, however, may be a function of (c)).

Cowgill concluded more simply, stating that prestige of the aged declines with increase in "modernization." Insofar as "modernization" implies shifts in the status structural determinants away from higher prestige generating poles, this generalization holds.

Certainly we must know more. For the present, at least, we believe that certain valid generalizations about status and prestige of the aged are now available. They are admittedly broad and hardly surprising in content. Few so-called social or cultural universals are otherwise. Hopefully, however, they will allow us to focus our attention more economically upon those areas of behavior which most directly affect the aged in all societies.

REFERENCES

Beals, Ralph. *Cheran: A Sierra Tarascan Village*. Institute of Social Anthropology, Publication 2. Washington, Smithsonian Institution, 1946.

Benedict, Ruth. Continuities and Discontinuities in Cultural Conditioning. *Psychiatry*. 1938, 1, 161-167.

Burgess, E. W. (ed.). *Aging in Western Societies*. Chicago: University of Chicago Press, 1960.

Cowgill, Donald. A Theoretical Framework for Considerations of Data on Aging. Paper delivered to the Society for Applied Anthropology, Miami, April, 1971.

Diaz, May N. *Tonala*. Berkeley: University of California Press, 1966.

Firth, Raymond. *We, the Tikopia*. Boston: Beacon Press, 1965.

[2] Manning Nash (1955) explicitly demonstrates how the introduction of civil elections has severely undermined a traditional civil-religious hierarchy in a Guatemalan community. Younger men had little opportunity for leadership in the past. Today they can by-pass the lengthy *cargo* sequence and stand for election to positions of leadership.

Foster, George M. *Tzintzuntzan*. Boston: Little Brown, 1967.

de la Fuente, Julio. *Yalalag: una villa zapoteca serrana*. An. of the Inst. Nacional de Antropologia e Historia, #1, Mexico, 1949.

Guiteras Holmes, Calixta. *Perils of the Soul: The World View of a Tzotzil Indian*. Glencoe: The Free Press, 1961.

Lansing, Albert I. General Biology of Senescence, in *Handbook of Aging and the Individual* (James E. Birren, ed.). Chicago: University of Chicago Press, 1959.

Lewis, Oscar. *Tepoztlan: Village in Mexico*. New York: Holt, Rinehart and Winston, 1960.

Nader, Laura. *Talea and Juquila: A Comparison of Zapotec*. Berkeley: University of California Publications in American Archaeology and Ethnology, 48, 195-296, 1964.

Nash, June. *In the Eyes of the Ancestors*. New Haven: Yale University Press, 1970.

Nash, Manning. *Machine Age Maya: the Industrialization of a Guatemalan Community*. Chicago: University of Chicago Press, 1969.

Nash, Manning. The Reaction of a Civil-Religious Hierarchy to a Factory in Guatemala. *Human Organization*. 1955, 13, 26-28.

Parsons, E. C. *Mitla: town of the Souls*. Chicago: University of Chicago Press, 1936.

Press, Irwin. Maya Aging: Cross-Cultural Projective Techniques and the Dilemma of Interpretation. *Psychiatry*. 1967, 30, 197-202.

Press, I., and Mike McKool, Jr. Social Structure and Status of the Aged in Peasant Society. Paper delivered to the Society for Applied Anthropology, Miami, April, 1971.

Reina, Ruben E. *The Law of the Saints*. Indianapolis: Bobbs-Merrill, 1966.

Romney, Kimball & Romaine. *The Mixtecans of Juxtlahuaca, Mexico*. New York: John Wiley, 1966.

Shanas, Ethel. Some Observations on Cross-National Surveys of Aging. *The Gerontologist*. 1963, 3, 7-9.

Shelton, Austin J. Ibo Aging and Eldership: Notes for Gerontologists and Others. *The Gerontologist*. 1965, 5, 20-23.

Simmons, Leo W. *The Role of the Aged in Primitive Society*. London: Oxford University Press, 1945.

Villa Rojas, Alfonso. *Notas sobre la etnografia de los Indios Tzeltales de Oxchuc*. Chicago: University of Chicago microfilm collection of Middle American cultural anthropology, #7, 1946.

Wolf, Eric. Closed, Corporate Peasant Communities in Meso-America and Central Java. *Southwestern Journal of Anthropology*. 1957, 13, 7-12.

Sons of the Shaking Earth. Chicago: University of Chicago Press, 1959.

chapter 4

THE CHANGING STATUS OF ELDERS IN A POLYNESIAN SOCIETY

Robert J. Maxwell

INTRODUCTION

ENOUGH has been written by anthropologists to indicate that the status of the aged varies greatly from society to society. Some familiar examples come to mind. The Siriono of the Bolivian highlands, like many nomadic hunters and gatherers, abandoned their aged and infirm without ceremony (Holmberg 1950). Similarly, certain inland Eskimo groups abandoned their old and sick, though this practice may not have been so widespread among the Eskimo as might be believed (Hughes 1961). The Chinese, on the other hand, venerated their aged, who were after all but one step removed from the guardians of the hearth, the ancestors. The *Li Chi,* or Book of Ritual, one of the classics of Chinese literature which political and social aspirants were required to learn, deals mostly with the care of the aged. And indeed, respect for the aged was so deeply ingrained in the Chinese that Gray (1878, p. 239) describes a law which, in the case of parricide, "expressly declares that not only shall the offender be subjected to a lingering death, but that the schoolmaster who instructed him in his youth shall be decapitated, and that the bones of his grandfathers shall be exhumed and scattered to the winds." Simmons' volume (1945), although methodologically faulty, suggests some of the determinants of the treatment of the aged. Case studies of how the aged fare abound (e.g., Arth 1965; Holmberg 1961; Shelton 1965; Smith 1961; Spencer 1965).

These studies, however valuable, are essentially synchronic. They have directed much attention to the status of the aged but relatively little to changes in that status as a result of contact with Western culture. The intent of this paper is to illustrate some of these changes as they occurred and are occurring now in Samoa, an island society in Western Polynesia. It will be suggested that the traditional authority of the elders has been undermined by a relatively recent influx of Western cultural and economic traits, particularly the introduction of a market exchange system.

SAMOAN SOCIAL STRUCTURE

It is necessary first to examine some aspects of the traditional social organization in order to provide a framework against which current developments may be viewed. The six larger islands of the Samoan group lie about fourteen degrees south of the equator and, all together, cover an area somewhat larger than 1200 square miles, or a bit larger than Rhode Island. The islands are not coral atolls; they are volcanic, mountainous, and rugged. They were settled by canoe-loads of voyagers from the west, perhaps at about the time of the flowering of classical Greece, 500 to 300 B.C. Like the Hawaiians, the people are racially polyglot: tall, brown-skinned, and robust.

Samoan subsistence originally depended upon the gathering of wild plant foods such as the coconut, the cultivation of roots and tubers, the raising of pigs and chickens, and the catching of fish and other sea animals. Their economy was in no sense specialized, although there was a division of labor between the sexes and between age groups, and, by the time of contact, such craftsmen as carpenters were beginning to emerge. Aside from occasional typhoons, which caused temporary shortages, the population was subject to no natural catastrophes and there was food enough for all.

The unit of kinship was the extended family, a group of relatives from both the male and female sides, who generally resided together in a group of thatch-roofed huts, along with other extended familites, in a single village. The village, then, consisted of several extended families, living side by side, and each family was headed by an elected chief. There were few absolute requirements for chieftainship, but ordinarily families were led by elderly men, rarely women, who were loyal to their kinsmen and socially skilled. When one was elected to chieftainship, he dropped his personal name and was addressed by his title instead. Titles varied considerably within the village in the degree of prestige accorded their holders. The more socially competent and economically successful chiefs acquired great political influence as representatives of their families at the village council.

A chief was normally succeeded by his oldest son, but arrangements for succession were quite flexible. The concern of paramount importance was the welfare of the family, and if the oldest son was not deemed qualified someone else was chosen. The prestige of a chief was expressed through the deference behavior of other villagers toward him. For example, at family gatherings, he was the first to be served kava, a spicy, mildly psychotropic beverage of ceremonial significance; he was the first served at feasts and was awarded the choicest parts of the pig. Those of lesser status were obliged to sit when he entered a room and to crouch and mutter apologies if they needed to walk past him or around him. Finally, if others addressed him, they used a ritualized, highly formal language with a rather different lexicon in order to indicate their respect, though it was impolite for a chief to use this ceremonial language when speaking about himself. If a chief was not shown proper respect, the slight was considered an insult by his entire family.

In return for all of this, a chief had dual responsibilities, as a member of his family on the one hand, and as a member of the village on the other. First, within the family itself, he acted as leader in the consideration of important family matters. He administered the land owned corporately by the extended family, deciding who should work which plots; he arbitrated family disputes; when necessary, he activated lesser chiefs' titles and assigned them to family members. In general, a chief saw to it that there was as much harmony and as little friction as possible between those who had elected him head of the family.

As a member of the village, he represented his family at the periodic meetings of the council of chiefs; he assumed his proper role in such cooperative community affairs as fishing, warfare, and the construction of community-owned buildings; and depending on his prestige, he arbitrated disputes between families and sometimes between villages. A chief had to play his role with deliberation (whether feigned or real), dignity, and a suitable acceptance and display of pomp.

The political and moral power of a chief, so far described, was underscored by his control over the exchange of valued material goods. The kind of control he exercised differed according to whether the exchange of goods was taking place within his own family or between his family and some other.

His extended family, of course, was made up of several conjugal units, each consisting of a man, his wife, their children, and perhaps other attached kinsmen. These conjugal units were largely in charge of their own subsistence affairs. They worked the land assigned to them, often fished and hunted by themselves, and raised their own domestic animals. Whenever anything resembling a surplus of food appeared as a result of their labors—following a fishing expedition, a crop harvest, or the killing of a pig—the conjugal unit was obliged to send a large portion of the surplus to the chief as an outright gift. The chief then set aside part of this for the use of his own wife and children, divided the rest into smaller portions, and sent these around to the other members of his extended family. He acted as a guidance mechanism, then, in the circulation of surplus food within the extended family.

In addition, there were occasions such as funerals, visits of large parties from other villages, and, later, church dedications, when enormous quantities of food and other materials were exchanged between extended families without the mediation of a superordinate figure of authority. If a villager from another family died, for example, it was a chief's duty to see that a suitable amount of valuable goods, such as finely woven mats, bark cloth, and food, were presented to the extended family of the dead person. It was the responsibility of the chief of the deceased's family to prepare an elaborate feast, during which quantities of food were given to the other families in the village. In other words, each extended family, under the leadership of its chief, was responsible only for its own performance at community ceremonies, and there was no overall figure in charge of the exchange.

The picture presented here is somewhat telescoped but is roughly accurate as a description of two models of sharing—between and within families. The former corresponds in some ways to what the economist Polanyi has called a reciprocal economy, the latter to a redistributive economy. It will be seen later how these are decaying under the impact of a recently introduced system of indirect exchange, dependent on the presence of money and markets (Polanyi, 1953).

Older women derived their status from that of their husbands. If a chief's wife did not have the political power of her husband, she nevertheless engaged in a substantial amount of backstage manipulation and her presence generated a similar kind of deference behavior in the villagers. When wives met for discussion, for example, they were served kava in the same order their husbands would have been served.

The exercise of this kind of power requires a certain minimum of physical vigor, but chiefs grow older like everyone else. A man might go on until he died in office. Or he might continue in office until he had grown so feeble that his authority was informally passed on to another family elder or to his oldest son. Grattan (1948, p. 15) describes another option open to an aging chief.

> Near the end of a long life of service for the family, a *matai* /chief/ may feel the burden of his position pressing too heavily upon his aged shoulders. He may then call his family together and after expressing his wish to retire from the burden of leadership, he may ask the family to choose some other holder of the title. . . . Thereafter, custom will permit him to take his usual place in the assembly of chiefs and orators without being troubled to any serious extent in respect of responsibility either as regards the family or the village. His cup will be distributed to him as usual in kava ceremonies. . . . Such a retired *matai* will wisely leave the greater part of the duties to his successor, putting forward an opinion occasionally without ostentation to help the new *matai*, who, if he wishes to win the approbation both of his predecessor and the village, will be careful from time time to show respect and recognition to the old man. And so the latter ends his days in peace and quietness, treated with that peculiar delicacy and consideration of which Samoan custom can be so pleasantly capable when the circumstances are favorable.

The infirm aged are cared for with matter-of-fact kindness within the family, mostly by women and older children. The unexpected death of a person in full vigor disrupts the social fabric, but death among the aged is accepted with some equanimity. The prevailing attitude in the aged is expressed in one elder's comment: "Why worry? When my time comes, I'll just lay down and go." This fatalistic attitude towards illness and death has been noticed by other observers (cf., Churchill, 1920).

There were distinctions between titled and untitled men and, of course, not every aged man was a chief. But elderly untitled men were still very much respected by the young, partly because of their accumulated wealth, their intrafamilial influence, their wisdom and experience, and because, simply put, they had survived into old age, a task not successfully accomplished by so many in the absence of modern medical care. In any case, despite distinctions, the desire to be a chief was universal, and with a record of continuing useful family service, a man's chances of being elected were good, so that the following statements, though dealing primarily with chiefs, may be taken as paradigmatic of the status of aged males in Samoa.

CONTACT WITH THE WEST

The Samoan Islands were discovered by the Dutch captain, Jacob Roggeveen, in 1722, but aside from occasional visits by Western ships, the islanders had little contact with Europeans or Americans until about 1830. This was rather late in the scheme of things, for by that time Hawaii had already undergone a great deal of culture change, and Tahiti, Tonga, and New Zealand were already being missionized. The delay is perhaps partly accounted for in terms of the fierce reputation the Samoans had acquired among early explorers.

In 1830, the ubiquitous preacher, John Williams, landed in Samoa. Meeting a powerful and accomodating chief, he and his colleagues rapidly converted the Samoans to Christianity. The social organization of the Samoans, who had never been terribly religious anyway, was little changed by the conversion. Following the missionary enterprises, there came a succession of American whalers, British colonials, and German traders. In 1900, the islands were divided, western Samoa going to Germany, eastern Samoa to America. In 1914, the western part came under the control of New Zealand and, in 1962, became the first country in Oceania to achieve independence. It is principally with the east part, where I spent twenty-two months conducting research in 1965 and 1966, that the remainder of this paper will be concerned.

American Samoa was ruled with relative benevolence by the Navy. Infrequent American ships used Pago Pago, with its fine harbor, as a coaling station. The small number of naval personnel were accepted at face value by the Samoans. Officers, with their elaborate ceremonial costumes, rituals, symbols of office, and so on, were understood to be chiefs, while the enlisted men were understood to be untitled. The Navy treated the chiefs with dignity, maintained dispensaries around the islands, and relationships were amicable. World War II saw a vast increase in the number of military personnel in the islands; more Western goods were introduced and certain native belief systems were so often violated by the Americans that they were taken under closer scrutiny by local leaders. (Everyone knew, for example, that ghosts were liable to attack and injure anyone walking alone through the jungle after dark, yet Marines stood solitary watch, unharmed, among the palm trees at night. Was it possible that ghosts were not as powerful as had been thought?)

None of this increase in the influx of Western traits had a great deal of impact on the basic structure of Samoan society itself, largely because the economic base remained the same. Authority still lay with the chiefs, who expected and received gifts of food and goods and who supervised the exchange of goods between families. The younger men provided the manpower, the older men supplied the guidance. After the war, the troops departed and the Samoans settled down into a life style more or less resembling that of their pre-war existence. Unknown to the majority of the populace, however, the last few years had created a framework within which an increasingly rapid rate of sociocultural change was to appear.

During the post-war period certain critical trends became apparent. First, transportation facilities were expanding rapidly. Roads around the largest island of Tutuila were being improved, so that people living in the outlying villages had greater access to the Pago Pago area, where most of the Americans and part-Samoans lived, and where wage work could be had and life had a decidedly more Western flavor.

Secondly, the population was becoming increasingly literate. Those who had learned little English in school had picked the language up from the troops. Many Samoans were now able to read the news bulletins and small newspapers which had been printed for years. The influence of reading material upon a culture that has previously had a strictly verbal tradition of passing on information cannot be over estimated. Older men and women, who had served the community as data banks, could now gradually be replaced by written archives. And, as if to facilitate the process of the replacement of the elderly, Western Samoa established its first radio broadcasting station in 1948, and American Samoa in 1952. Programs were as much concerned with instruction in tasks like horticulture as they were with entertainment, a further incursion into the pool of data controlled by the older and more experienced members of the community (cf., Keesing and Keesing, 1954, p. 156–82; Roberts, 1964).

Finally, material items of Western culture came to have a greater impact on Samoan life. Those items dealing merely with the storage of food were of enormous importance. Foodsharing customs can be partly explained in ecological terms, the climate of Samoa being such that food spoiled quickly unless consumed. (The only significant food especially prepared for storage was a kind of tough biscuit of fermented breadfruit, typically made following a typhoon which knocked down many of the breadfruit trees anyway.) The food given to others, however, was not forever gone. Sooner or later, others would have a surplus and would return a like amount. The effect was that one's neighbors acted as storage bins for food.

The family chiefs were the most important figures in the circulation of food within the village, and they extracted a share for the consumption of their own conjugal famililies. But with the increasing post-war exposure to varieties of canned goods and dried foods like rice, there was less incentive to share one's food with others. And with the introduction of the refrigerator, following electrification of the more remote communities, food exchange was further slowed. As a result, not only was the chief given fewer outright gifts of food, but he was denied the share he would have received had food exchange continued at its pre-war pace.

The naval administration was dissolved in 1951 and the territory transferred to the Department of the Interior. The new administration changed little in the formal political organization of Samoan society. Under the Governor of American Samoa, the chiefs held as much political and legal power as before. (To be sure, the governor was empowered to overrule any law the chiefs might enact, and to ignore any suggestions they might make, but he generally exercised more subtle means of control.)

However, in 1964 the government revamped the entire educational system, consolidating the schools at every level, thereby eliminating many poorly run elementary schools in outlying districts, and introduced a highly structured system of education television. At about the same time, a multi-million dollar hotel was constructed in the Pago Pago area, providing wage work for hundreds of young Samoan men and women. The hotel is now staffed entirely by Samoans and part-Samoans except for the manager. A recently constructed jet airstrip and modern airport likewise opened new opportunities for work.

In 1962, there were 5,833 Samoans and part-Samoans engaged in wage work. The majority of these were government employees. This number constitutes 42%

of the available labor force, including both males and females (American Samoa Governor's Report: 1962). And since the completion of the hotel and the construction of the new airport and the consolidated schools, the number of Samoans with wage-work experience has gone up considerably. This is undoubtedly a secular or long-term trend. Wage work and the regular bi-weekly pay check are indispensable parts of most households today.

All other sources of subsistence seem to be declining in importance, even though there are important financial rewards for the adults who systematically work their family gardens, called "plantations." At the open marketplace in Pago Pago, for example, one may buy local produce—taro, yam, bananas, and pineapples—at relatively high prices. Pineapples that might cost 49¢ in an American supermarket cost 75¢ in the marketplace. The demand is greater than the supply, so that some of this produce must be imported from Western Samoa and elsewhere. However, the plantations are not used to their capacity because Western foods are becoming more important and because more of the young adults are staying in school, working locally for wages, or migrating elsewhere, and so they are unable to provide the labor necessary for the exploitation of the land.

Furthermore, there seems to be a selective recruitment of wage-workers from among the younger and more ambitious people. Most wage work in Samoa consists of manual labor— construction, maintenance, road work, and so forth— under a blazing tropical sun, six days a week, for a starting wage of about 45¢ an hour. These jobs are not for the elderly or the lazy. One could stay at home, working his plantation pretty much when he felt like it, and still provide food for his family. Some do exactly this, but they are mostly the elderly, or the less Westernized young adults.

Similarly, many of the more talented young men and women are completing high school and entering institutions of higher learning, either in the local teacher-training schools or in colleges and universities in the United States. By 1966, for example, the Government of American Samoa had sent 110 students abroad on scholarships, in addition to those students being supported by their families (reported in the Samoan Times, April 4, 1966). And greater numbers of working young people are emigrating to America simply because wages, and the life style, are higher there.

Those who live abroad send some part of their pay to their parents and to their family chiefs, just as they would have shared their fishing catches. Whether distant sons support their families with the same enthusiasm as they would if they were still living at home cannot be determined. But in any case, since this transfer of wealth does not take place as part of a face-to-face interaction, the sender need not feel so embarrassed if the gift is a bit smaller than it might be. And furthermore the chief has no way of knowing exactly how bountiful the emigrant's catch was.

DISCUSSION

The impingement of Western culture on Samoan life has become pronounced since World War II and especially since the transfer of the territory to the Department of the Interior in 1951. This impingement has become apparent through the expansion of facilities for transportation, communication, and education, all of which have exposed young Samoans to American concepts of autonomy and private property, and which have rendered the elderly increasingly less useful as information sources. The influence of American culture on Samoan life is also evident in the introduction of items that facilitate the storage of food, and in the increasing dependence of the Samoan family and the economy in general upon wages, earned primarily by younger people.

What is the effect of all this on the status of elders in Samoa? Two examples may help make the impact of these continuing changes clearer. The first is taken directly from an interview recorded in the field. The informant is a man in his mid-twenties, a graduate of a small college in the United States, currently a teacher in one of the consolidated high schools. His statements are fairly typical for a young man of his background.

Q: *Woud you like to have a title?*

A: Title? Oh, you mean a chief title? No. I sure would like to get rid of this chief system.

Q: *Why?*

A: It seems to me that the chiefs of the clans are taking advantage of the people who don't hold titles. Nowadays some of the young people are getting used to some of the Western ideas. It used to be that everybody in the family would work and give their whole pay check to the chief, and he would distribute the money to the members of the family. But I would like to work and give the money away the way I want. I would not give it to the chief to distribute. Maybe fifty years ago, if somebody went fishing, he would come back and give all the fish to the chief. And the chief would distribute them. But now, if I want to go fishing, I don't give any to the chief. If I want to eat them all, I eat them all. My family has asked me several times to try to get a title, and I say: "No—my name is Va'afatu Tupiano, and I'll die being Va'afatu Tupiano!" Sometimes the chief doesn't know anything. Sometimes people want to change things and the Samoans say, "Let's not. It's tradition." But I think if it's for the good of the people, a change should be made. I'm not afraid of change. The old people do not like their children to go to American dances. I don't know anything about Amerian dancing, but I say if they want to go, let them go.

Another of my informants, a man of 36 who worked in the Pago Pago area, was approached in my presence by an older kinsman. The younger man, Peter, asked the old man, Ulu, to sit down and join us. Ulu did so. He was a chief, albeit a minor chief, and he curled his legs under him on the floor mat, smoothed the folds of his loincloth, and bending his cropped and grizzled head, spoke slowly and with dignified deliberation about the responsibilities of chieftainship. Peter nodded his head and listened earnestly, waiting for the old man to finish. Ulu finally put it to Peter that there was a vacancy in one of the titles of the family and, since he knew Peter to be industrious and loyal, he would very much like Peter to think about assuming the title and becoming a chief himself. Peter politely thanked him for being so generous in his judgements, but pointed out that he had spent several years in the Coast Guard, and several years following that working in Honolulu. These experiences, Peter said, had given him too many new ideas for him to perform very well as a chief. He pointed out that there were other men in the family who were older and more tradition-oriented than he was and therefore more suitable to become head of the family.

When Ulu had gone, Peter turned to me and grimaced. "I don't want none of that chief stuff! Who cares about chief anymore?" He went on to say that in his village—in which there were about eighteen chiefs—only one family shared its food with the chief the way they did in the old days. The other families still tendered gifts of food and goods to their chiefs, but not the way they used to. The chief had all sorts of responsibilities; he had to worry all the time and he couldn't get drunk at parties, but he received too little in return.

Peter was talking about the irrelevance of the elders, and about the discrepancy between the allocation of economic power, accruing more and more to the young, and political power, which still rested formally in the hands of the elderly. Family heads, who previously commanded the distribution of wealth, now find themselves with a decreasing economic basis for their political authority. And they themselves are not unaware that their power is being threatened from many sides. One of the reasons they opposed the government-sponsored house-building program following the typhoon of 1966 is that they feared they would lose their authority over the administration of the land (editorial, Samoan *Times*, May 9, 1966).

And their moral influence, even within their own families, is waning, as more youngsters move out from under their scrutiny and control and establish themselves as wage earners elsewhere. (An added difficulty is that these restless young men are precisely those who, at the time of contact, would have been bold and daring warriors, owing allegiance to no control agent higher than the head of the family. Lost in the anonymity of an urban setting, they cause a disproportionate amount of trouble. A Honolulu newspaper recently conducted a survey of forty-three Samoan households in Hawaii in an attempt to discover some of the reasons for this.)

The feedback within the system is positive. The more young wage earners control the flow of wealth, the more incentive there is for other young people to enter wage work themselves. These generalizations have been phrased in qualitative terms, but there is empirical evidence elsewhere that the introduction of money and wage-work into the economy of Samoan villages is associated with the decay of the traditional power structure (Ember, 1964). And there are suggestions that the processes outlined here are not restricted to Polynesia but have occurred among such widely different people as urban Chinese (Yap, 1962), the isolated Havasupai of Arizona (Smithson, 1959, p. 130), and the cattleherding Hottentot of South Africa (Schultze, 1907, p. 102).

Nothing here is meant to imply that Samoan elders—chiefs or otherwise—are treated contemptuously. Indeed, the opposite is true. Younger persons, whatever work they are engaged in and wherever they are located, unfailingly contribute money and other gifts to the family through the chief, and they invariably show respect for elders in direct encounters. However, the suggestion of this paper is that recent developments in a situation of culture contact have undermined the traditional authority of elders in Samoa and has made them less functional as controllers of information and wealth. With the ongoing Americanization of the islands and their peoples, this trend is likely to continue.

REFERENCES

American Samoa Governor's Report to the Secretary of the Interior. GPO, Washington, 1962.

Arth, M. J. The Role of the Aged in a West African Village. *Gerontologist,* 5, Part 2, p. 43, 1965.

Churchill, L. P. *Samoa 'Uma.* Sampson, Low, Marsten, and Co., London, 1920.

Ember, M. Commercialization and Political Change in American Samoa, *in* W. Goodenough (Ed.), *Explorations in Cultural Anthropology,* McGraw-Hill, New York, 1964.

Grattan, F. J. H. An Introduction to Samoan Custom. Samoa Printing and Publishing Co.. Ltd., Apia, 1948.

Gray, J. H. *China: A History of the Laws, Manners, and Customs of the People* I. MacMillan, London, 1878.

Holmberg, A. R. Age in the Andes, *in* R. W. Kleemeier, (ed.), *Aging and Leisure,* Oxford Univ. Press, New York, 1961.

Holmberg, A. R. *Nomads of the Long Bow.* Smithsonian Inst. Soc. Anthrop., Washington, Publication No. 10, 1950.

Hughes, C. C. The Concept and Use of Time in the Middle Years: the St. Lawrence Island Eskimo, *in* R. W. Kleemeier (ed.), *Aging and Leisure,* Oxford Univ. Press, New York, 1961.

Keesing, F. M. and M. M. Keesing. *Elite Communication in Samoa: A Study of Leadership.* Stanford Univ. Press, Stanford, 1956.

Li Chi (The Book of Ritual). Translated by James Legge. Sacred Books of the East, Oxford, 1879-85.

Polanyi, K. *Semantics of General Economic History.* (Rev. Ed.) Columbia Univ. Research, New York. Project on "Origins of Economic Institutions" 1953.

Roberts, J. M. The self-management of cultures, *in* W. Goodenough (Ed.) *Explorations in Cultural Anthropology,* McGraw-Hill, New York, 1964.

Schultze, L. *Aus Namaland und Kalahari.* Jena. Translated and incorporated into the Human Relations Area Files, 1907.

Shelton, A. J. Ibo Aging and Eldership: Notes for Gerontologists and Others. *Gerontologist,* 5, pp. 20-3, 1965.

Simmons, L. W. *The Role of the Aged in Primitive Society.* Yale Univ. Press, New Haven, 1945.

Smith, R. J. Cultural Differences in the Life Cycle and the Concept of Time, *in* R. W. Kleemeier (ed.), *Aging and Leisure,* Oxford Univ. Press, New York, 1961.

Smithson, C. The Havasupai Woman. *Anthropological Papers,* Univ. of Utah, 1959.

Spencer, P. *The Samburu: A Study of Gerontocracy in a Nomadic Tribe.* Univ. of California Press, Berkeley and L.A., 1965.

Yap, P. M. Aging in Underdeveloped Asian Countries, *in* C. Tibbitts and W. Donahue, *Social and Psychological Aspects of Aging: Aging Around the World.* Columbia Univ. Press, New York, 1962.

chapter 5

PRESTIGE OF THE AGED IN PORTUGAL: REALISTIC APPRAISAL AND RITUALISTIC DEFERENCE*

Aaron Lipman

THIS paper attempts to assess the differences in prestige rankings of the aged in contemporary Portugal, and to place this information in a crosscultural gerontological perspective. Pursuing this objective also involves an effort to operationalize the concept of "prestige of the elderly".

Until very recently the degree of prestige accorded the elder members of a social grouping had been viewed stereotypically as being higher in *Gemeinschaft* than in *Gesellschaft* forms of social organization. Gerontologists postulated that as urbanization increased the high social prestige of the elderly concurrently diminished. This view has been questioned; doubt has arisen as to whether the aged have ever enjoyed the high prestige we believed they once were accorded. Thus, in a comparative study of ancient Greeks, Hebrews, and Romans, Koller (1968) found that there was a tendency to idealize the attitudes toward and treatment of the older part of the population; the reality was not so idyllic. The same held true for both elderly medieval Europeans as well as elderly colonial Americans.

A study by Harlan (1964) of three Indian villages also throws doubt on the long-held belief that the aged were ascribed uniformly high prestige in sacred, traditionalistic milieus, but somehow lost it through drastic changes imposed by a modern more secular society. He granted that urbanization and industrialization bring about changes in kinship and family organizational patterns, but denied that the aged as a category suffered the loss of their formerly high social status.

Neugarten's (1967) statement probably reflects the contemporary position. She observes: "There is reason to doubt . . . that in earlier times, either in Western or non-Western societies, the aged were uniformly valued as a group. Their status has probably always had both positive and negative elements . . ."

While in Portugal as a Fulbright Professor the author undertook to unravel the apparent conflict between these propositions by comparing respondents from

*Revised version of paper presented at the 8th International Congress of Gerontology, Washington, D.C., August 24–29, 1969. Research was supported by a National Science Foundation Institutional Grant (GU2151) to the University of Miami.

Lisbon, one of the most highly industrialized and urbanized centers in Portugal, with respondents from three primitive northwest districts (Vila Real, Guarda, and Branganca) with respect to their attitudes about the aged segment of their population.

Portugal, representing one of the underdeveloped nations of Western Europe, still has some remote areas that have not been very much affected by urbanization or industrialization; these areas would presumably be representative of traditionalistic or rural Portuguese attitudes and behavior patterns. Since the population of Portugal is relatively stable and the country is quite small, a further implicit assumption is that as industrialization becomes more widespread, these remote areas will undergo an evolutionary change similar to that of Lisbon (although, admittedly, we certainly would expect an international seaport to differ in many ways from any inland city, no matter how urbanized). It was anticipated that, for Portugal, the comparison between rural and urban dwellers represented the closest reflection possible of a *Gemeinschaft-Gesellschaft* distinction employing a contemporary model.

Urban societies characteristically exhibit a universalistic achievement orientation. These value orientations .tend to diminish the status of the aged person, since he is no longer judged by particularistic criteria and must compete in the achievement struggle with younger individuals who have obvious advantages. It was therefore hypothesized that rural dwellers would hold the aged in more esteem than would urban dwellers.

Lisbon is the most accessible urban center in Portugal, ranking first in practically all indices of transportation and means of communication, as well as level of urbanization. Whereas Lisbon ranks highest in the number of installed telephones per 1,000 residents, for example, Branganca ranks lowest. No newspaper is published in either Guarda and Branganca; further, these two areas rank lowest in the number of radios per 1,000 residents. Table 1 compares the levels of urbanization of the five above mentioned districts, using as indices the number of telephones, newspapers, movies, radios, television sets, automobile and electrical energy consumed/per 1,000 inhabitants. Of the eighteen districts in Portugal, Lisbon ranks first, Guarda ranks fourteenth, Vila Real fifteenth, and Braganca eighteenth, or last. If urbanization is indexed by the percentage of Portugal's population living in centers of 5,000 or more inhabitants, Braganca has a 3.6 level, Vila Real a 8.2 level, and Guarda a 2.5 level of urbanization. In the rural districts the industrial labor force (as a percent of the active population) is less than half that of Lisbon. (Pintado, 1964) Finally, as compared to Lisbon, the life expectancy of the population is these other districts is about five years less than that of the population of Lisbon. (Centro de Estudios de Economia Agraria, 1963)

PROCEDURE

The rural respondents were selected from rural provinces of Portugal, while the urban sample was drawn from people living in Lisbon, Portugal. The 183 urban dwellers, and the 317 rural dwellers fall into the same modal age category, that of 20-29. Similarly, the largest percentages of both urban and rural samples were married at the time they were interviewed, although a significant percentage of each sample was found to be single. We might note here that there was a larger percentage of rural dwellers than urban dwellers listing themselves as having been widowed (6.0% as compared to 1.6%). This is probably due to the larger percentage of older respondents in the rural sample than in the urban sample. Examining the educational level attained by our respondents, we found that educational attainment tends to be higher for urban dwellers than for our rural sample. As we would suspect, the only category of educational attainment which veers even slightly from the hypothesized tendency is that of Commercial-Industrial-Agricultural Institute attendance. As we would expect, the urban dwellers have had Commercial and Industrial training, while the rural respondents who have attained this level have attended agriculture Institute classes. Below is a table summarizing the background material for our samples.

THE SAMPLE

A purposive selection and abstraction of value criteria permits their operationalization with empirical referents, thus allowing us to compare empirical

TABLE 1

Urban Industrial Indicators

District	1	2	3	4	5	6	7	8	9
	Means of Communication					Means of Transportation		Level of Urbanization	Consumption of electric energy
	Telephone	Newspapers	Movies	Radio	Television	Auto Vehicles			
						Heavy	Light		
Lisbon	116.4	437.4	11.2	222.4	6.1	5.30	38.20	71.2	158
Braganca	8.6	—	0.3	18.5	0.2	1.60	5.20	3.6	5
Guarda	10.2	—	0.5	31.4	0.6	1.80	7.50	2.5	28
Villa Real	11.9	3.7	0.6	30.3	0.4	1.40	6.10	8.2	25
Continent	35.7	102.1	3.5	91.1	2.1	—	—	24.6	71

1) Per 1000 inhabitants
2) 1000 newspapers per 1000 inhabitants
3) 1000 spectators per 1000 inhabitants
4) Number per 1000 inhabitants
5) Number per 1000 inhabitants
6) Per 1000 inhabitants
7) Per 1000 inhabitants
8) Percentage of population in centers of 5000 or more inhabitants
9) Killowatt hours per inhabitant

Source: Niveis de Desenvolvimento agricola no Continente Portugues. Lisbon 1963, Centro de Estudios de Economia Agraria. pp. 238–9.

TABLE 2

Characteristics of the Urban and Rural Samples

Sex	Urban		Rural	
	No.	Pct.	No.	Pct.
Male	99	34.1	213	67.2
Female	84	45.9	104	32.5
Age				
10–19	11	6.0	17	5.4
20–29	84	45.9	79	24.9
30–39	30	16.4	61	19.2
40–49	28	15.3	59	18.6
50–59	22	12.0	47	14.8
60+	8	4.4	53	16.7
Marital Status				
Single	83	45.4	129	40.7
Married	93	50.8	166	52.4
Widowed	3	1.6	19	6.0
Other	4	2.2	2	.6
Educational Attainment				
None-Primary	69	37.7	233	73.5
Secondary/Technical	53	29.0	49	15.5
Commercial/Industrial				
Agriculture Institute	15	8.2	23	7.3
University	46	25.1	12	3.8

data. Both enumeration of prevalence and measurement of intensity are sub-components of comparison; the scale developed by the author was intended as a heuristic device which might serve in the future as a base for the measurement and comparison of prestige of the aged. Whereas the structural components of behavior have been studied previously (Harlan, 1964), the present study adapts and applies quantifying techniques to attitudinal-cognnitive components of behavior.

Age was randomly represented in the final selection of the total sample of the five hundred. The various districts were sampled, with each district represented as follows; 118 from Guarda, 100 from Braganca, 99 from Vila Real, and 183 from Lisbon. Sixteen statements were presented to both rural and urban subjects, who were asked to respond to the five alternative Agree-Disagree items. Depending on the direction of the statement (i.e., negative or positive), a response of "Strongly Agree" or "Strongly Disagree" was scored as 5, "Agree" or "Disagree" was scored as 4, etc. It was therefore possible to determine a mean score of agreement for each statement and for each district. The higher the score, the greater should be the prestige ascribed the elderly. The maximum score obtainable was 5 while the minimum was 1. Critical ratios were determined in order to test for statistically significant differences between the mean scores for the rural and Lisbon populations. Internal consistency and unidimensionality of the scale items were tested by the use of the factor analysis technique.

FINDINGS

With the exception of their standing on a few statements, urban and rural respondents tended to agree in their assessment of the position the elderly of the society occupy. However, the proportion of each sample agreeing with the statements, as well as the intensity of the agreement/disagreement varied widely, and between the rural and Lisbon respondents was statistically significant. By combining the "strongly agree," " agree" categories and the "strongly disagree," "disagree" categories we can see that the majority of both urban and rural subsamples with the folowing statements:

> One should always give up one's seat to an old person. (Item 11)
> Old people know more about the world than others because they have had more experience. (Item 14)
> Old age is the worst time of life. (Item 18)
> In our society old people are useful. (Item 21)
> Old people are too old-fashioned. (Item 22)
> One should always consult an old person before making any important decisions. (Item 25)

A closer examination of the data in Table 3, however, shows that there was a large enough difference between the mean scores of items 14, 18, 21, and 25 to be significant at the .001 level. In addition the critical ratio of the difference between the rural and urban means for item 22 was significant at the .05 level.

In a similar fashion, the majority of both the urban and rural groups *disagreed* that:

> In our society an old person is not important. (Item 12)
> An old person may just as well be dead. (Item 15)
> The old person can expect much from the future. (Item 19)
> The world should be governed by old people. (Item 24)

Furthermore, Table 3 indicates the mean differences among response categories of Items 15 and 24 to be significant at the .001 level; among response categories of Item 12 the difference was significant at the .05 level. The mean scores of Item 24 showed no significant difference.

In addition there were a number of items where there was a divergence of direction between the responses of urban and rural subjects. Thus more urban respondents, in contrast to rural respondents, *agreed* that:

> Old people are a burden on society. (Item 23)
> Most people just pretend that they like old people. (Item 13)

Most Lisbon, as compared to the more rural, respondents, *disagreed* that:

> Old people hold back progress. (Item 26)

The large majority of rural respondents, as compared to a smaller majority of Lisbon respondents, believed that:

> One should not contradict an old person, even when he is wrong. (Item 20)
> It is the fate of the old to suffer. (Item 16)

Although there was no clearcut distinction between rural and urban respondents for statement 17, 42% of the rural population agreed, and 49% of the urban population agreed with this statement, showing a tendency in the predicted direction:

> The joys of being old are highly overrated. (Item 17)

TABLE 3

Mean Scores, Standard Errors, Critical Ratios and Significance Levels of Attitude Statements Toward the Aged

Attitude Statement	Rural N=317			Mean Score		Lisbon N=183			Mean Score		Critical Ratio of Difference
	A %	U %	D %			A %	U %	D %			
11) One should always give up one's seat to an old person.	98.7	.3	.9	4.9	0.45	88.0	3.3	8.7	4.4	1.05	5.9382***
12) In our society an old person is not important.	16.4	6.9	76.7	4.0	1.25	18.6	11.5	69.9	3.8	1.19	1.9627*
13) Most people just pretend they like old people.	43.2	23.0	33.8	2.9	1.26	56.3	11.5	32.2	2.6	1.25	2.9013**
14) Old people know more about the world than others because they have had more experience.	70.7	8.5	20.8	3.9	1.35	55.2	12.6	32.2	3.4	1.38	4.6253***
15) An old person may just as well be dead.	25.9	12.9	61.2	3.6	1.29	8.7	3.3	88.0	4.3	0.99	7.2239***
16) It is the fate of the old to suffer.	63.1	9.1	27.8	2.5	1.35	31.1	12.0	56.3	3.4	1.40	8.2872***
17) The joys of being old are highly overrated.	42.0	25.9	32.2	2.9	1.14	49.7	18.0	32.2	2.7	1.22	1.9920*
18) Old age is the worst time of life.	79.8	10.1	10.1	1.8	1.09	55.7	10.4	33.9	2.5	1.46	6.5851***
19) The old person can expect much from the future.	6.9	6.9	86.1	1.8	0.98	8.7	6.6	84.7	1.8	0.94	No difference
20) One should not contradict an old person, even when he is wrong.	68.1	6.9	24.9	3.8	1.37	40.4	9.8	49.7	2.8	1.39	9.2081***
21) In our society, old people are useful.	77.3	9.8	12.9	4.0	1.10	56.3	23.0	20.8	3.5	1.10	5.1599***
22) Old people are too old fashioned.	58.4	20.5	21.1	2.5	1.15	50.8	17.5	31.7	2.7	1.19	1.9920*
23) Old people are a burden on society.	37.9	14.2	47.9	3.2	1.35	22.4	7.7	69.9	3.6	1.19	3.8684***
24) The world should be governed by old people.	29.7	16.7	53.6	2.6	1.47	14.2	13.7	72.1	2.0	1.20	5.6980***
25) One should always consult an old person before making any important decisions.	81.7	6.6	11.7	4.1	1.08	60.1	8.2	31.7	3.4	1.37	6.7372***
26) Old people hold back progress.	38.5	22.7	38.8	3.1	1.30	30.1	12.0	57.9	3.4	1.24	2.8873**

*Significant at the .05 level

**Significant at the .01 level

***Significant at the .001 level

Internal consistency and uni-dimensionality of the scale items were tested by the use of the factor analysis technique. Factor analysis, it might be noted, is a statistical method of examining the degree to which intercorrelations among related items are basically manifestations of the same single dimension or underlying factor. A correlation matrix indicates the intercorrelation among all the items; these items are then clustered by the factor loading procedure.

The degree of relationship between each item and the underlying factor or dimension is expressed by this factor loading, which can range from —1.0 to 1.0.

TABLE 4

Varimax Rotation of Attitudinal Items

	1	2	3	4	5
		Per cent of Variance			
	16.927	14.768	7.767	8.127	6.654
		Rotated Factor Loadings			
11	0.381	—0.187	—0.038	0.357	—0.431
12	0.093	0.103	—0.137	0.787	0.033
13	0.126	—0.074	0.324	0.610	0.116
14	0.620	0.033	0.018	0.107	—0.074
15	—0.336	0.644	—0.258	0.196	—0.029
16	—0.487	0.565	0.011	—0.015	0.001
17	0.079	0.018	—0.019	0.183	0.831
18	—0.333	0.484	0.360	0.129	—0.079
19	—0.058	0.067	0.870	0.029	—0.013
20	0.683	—0.160	—0.166	0.113	0.046
21	0.404	0.397	0.162	0.128	—0.228
22	0.185	0.507	0.274	—0.076	0.244
23	—0.066	0.778	—0.070	—0.017	—0.062
24	0.716	0.085	0.104	—0.109	0.153
25	0.702	—0.119	—0.045	0.165	—0.018
26	0.099	0.320	0.132	—0.080	0.145

From Table 4, we can see that 16.9% of the variations are associated with the first factor, and 14.8% of the variations are associated with the second factor (54% of the variations are associated with five factors).

The scale items dichotomized into two discrete dimensions; these were respectively designated Factors 1 and 2. The Items of Factor 1 exemplified by "One should not contradict an old person, even when he is wrong," are positive statements, and taken as a distinct dimension seem to be associated with power, authoritarianism, and the deference accorded groups who possess or exercise these attributes. When juxtaposed with the items of Factor 2, however, a different interpretation becomes patient. The items of Factor 2, exemplified by "An Old Person May Just As Well Be Dead," are negative statements, which represent old age as a highly undesirable time of life. On the surface, Factors 1 and 2 seem to be incompatible or contradictory, and their co-existence problematic. This difficulty disappears, however, if the factor common to all statements of Factor 2 is conceptualized as a reflection of the real objective appraisal by publics of the aged condition, while the factor common to all the statements of Factor 1 reflects not actual, but *ritual* deference, a kind of "lip service" paid to the idea of honoring the aged.

Tables 5 and 6 also show that the percentage of agreement with *all* ritual deference positive items common to Factor 1 and with *all* realistic appraisal negative items common to Factor 2 was significantly higher for the rural group (representative of a *Gemeinschaft* orientation) than for the urban (*Gesellschaft*)

TABLE 5

FACTOR 1—Ritual Deference

		Percentage of Respondents Agreeing	
Factor Loading	Item	Rural	Lisbon
.620	Old people know more about the world than others because they have had more experience.	70.7%	55.2%
.683	One should not contradict an old person, even when he is wrong.	68.1%	40.4%
.716	The world should be governed by old people.	29.7%	14.2%
.702	One should always consult an old person before making any important decisions.	81.7%	30.1%

TABLE 6

FACTOR 2—Realistic Appraisal

		Percentage of Respondents Agreeing	
Factor Loading	Item	Rural	Lisbon
.644	An old person may just as well be dead.	25.9%	8.7%
.565	It is the fate of the old to suffer.	63.1%	31.7%
.484	Old age is the worst time of life.	79.8%	55.7%
.507	Old people are too old fashioned.	68.1%	40.4%
.778	Old people are a burden on society.	37.9%	22.4%
.520	Old people hold back progress.	38.5%	30.1%

respondents. Even where the direction of response was the same, significant differences appeared in the intensity of responses of rural respondents as contrasted with the intensity of those of urban residents.

CONCLUSION AND DISCUSSION

When rural and urban population samples, representing the closest approximation to a *Gemeinschaft-Gesellschaft* contrast possible in contemporary Portugal, were administered an old-age attitude scale, two salient findings emerged: first, while the general direction of most responses was the same for both subsamples there were significant differences in the degree or intensity of agreement. Secondly, the concept "position of the aged" emerged as a composite of (at least) two dimensions. Factor 1, the positive component, has been designated *ritual deference,* while Factor 2, the negative component, is assumed to represent *realistic appraisal.* These concepts are theoretically as well as statistically relevant.

The conceptual construct *ritual deference* might do much to explain the unremitting persistence of the myth that old people enjoyed high prestige in the traditionalistic *Gemeinschaft* society. Ritual deference in this instance would be the normative manifestation of behavior that seems to honor old people. The value system of the society posits that old people are to be treated as if they were wise and respected, on the basis of their age alone. The respect thus accorded them, however, turns out to be mostly a matter of ritual form. (Ritualism of all kinds tends to be higher in a *Gemeinschaft* society). In other words a young man might say, "One should seek the advice of older people, because they have a great deal of experience," and then not do so. Or he might seek and receive advice from an old person, and then not follow it. Arensberg and Kimball (1968), who speak about the high prestige accorded the aged in a traditional society, give an example of this "lip service" aspect of ritual deference, when they describe a farmer who listened patiently and politely to his aged father's orders, and then followed his own devices in actually running the farm. The same authors also describe situations where, although ritual deference was accorded older men to their faces, behind their backs they were held to be "old fools."

We find strong hints of this situation emerging from the interstices of other studies of traditionalistic society that purport to prove how high a status old people enjoyed in former times. Simmons (1945) states, for example, that "Most primitive societies have insured some respect for the aged . . . but under close analysis, respect for old age has, as a rule, been accorded to persons on the basis of some particular asset which they possessed." Even the old Irish countrymen described by Arensberg and Kimball derived their positions directly from their control of land, of marriage, and of occupational inheritance, i.e., personal resources—rather than solely as a function of advanced age.

Harlan (1964) found the same conditions in the Indian villages he studied. Old age was not the basis by which informal or formal leadership was accorded. Instead, leadership seemed to be correlated with attributes such as socio-economic status and education. "Insofar as older men occupy positions of leadership in affairs beyond those of the family, they do so in consequence of attributes other than chronological age."

In traditional societies it seems then, that real power, prestige, and authority were not necessarily associated with advanced age *per se.* Power, prestige or authority were acquired through the regular channels of the status hierarchy, namely, on the basis of the individual's attributes and resources, and were the same for old men as they were for young ones. What was accorded the aged as a group, however, was ritual deference. This seems to happen in much the same way that a nation espousing liberty as part of its value system can at the same time tolerate repression, or a society that can condemn violence on one hand, can simultaneously institutionalize war on the other.

The actual physical conditions of life in the *Gemeinschaft* community are much harder than the physical conditions in the *Gesellschaft* society. Ill health and economic strain may be two pivotal factors that affect old people as a group; both of these factors tend to improve significantly the advent of industrialization. Technology reduces the portion of a man's adult years necessary for work, and at the same time reduces the physical exertion expended; medical advances help keep health from failing. With few exceptions, industrialization has brought with it a concomitant rise in living standards. Factor 2 of the present study, the realistic appraisal of the situation of the aged, showed an understandable diminution in the percentage of urban people viewing old age in completely negative terms. It is suggested that this diminishment in the completely negative stereotype of old age is a reflection of the reality of a rising standard of living and the fact that old age becomes less of a physical handicap.

In the course of this investigation, then, "degree of prestige of the aged" was found to be at least a two-dimensional concept, involving both realistic appraisal and ritual deference. Future gerontological research should, it is suggested, continue to concentrate on isolating and identifying further specific components of "prestige of the aged" in other cultural areas under study.

REFERENCES

Arensberg, C. M., and Kimball, S. T., *Family and community in Ireland*. (2nd Ed.) Harvard University Press, Cambridge, 1968.

Centro de Estudos de Economia Agraria. *Niveis de desenvolvimento agricola no continente portugues*. Imprensa Nacional, Lisbon, 1963.

Harlan, W. H. Social Status of the aged in three indian villages. *Vita Humane*, 7, 239–52, 1964.

Koller, M. R. *Social gerontology*. Random House, New York, 1968.

Neugarten, B. L. The aged in american society. In H. S. Becker (Ed.), *Social problems: a modern approach*. John Wiley & Sons, New York, 1967.

Pintado, V. X. *Structure and growth of the portuguese economy*. European Free Trade Association, Geneva, 1964.

Simmons, L. W. *The role of the aged in primitive society*. Yale University Press, New Haven, 1945.

chapter 6

ATTITUDES TOWARD THE ELDERLY IN SWEDEN: CORRELATES AND AGE GROUP COMPARISONS

John Skoglund

Since the empirical research of Tuckman, Lorge, and their associates initially directed the interest of gerontologists toward the study of perceptions of old age [1-3], American investigators have reported generally, but not entirely, negative stereotypes among young and middle-aged adults. Old age is regarded as markedly different from earlier years, a period of life characterized by passivity, social withdrawal, and isolation for reviews of the literature [4, 5].

During the past decade or so there has been a shift in research strategies away from instruments covering various categories of misconceptions, erroneous views, and undesirable personal traits. Accompanied by methodological refinements there has been an increasing interest in multidimensional investigations of the factorial structure of attitudes toward old people and old age

[4-7]. The scope of conceptualization regarding the attitudinal referent, how-ever, has regularly been restricted to "old people."

By way of contrast to the latter point, the attitudes investigated in the present study are concerned with issues of rather pragmatical applications in terms of perceptions of activities and societal relations thought to be of rele-vance for the elderly. In a previous report, I investigated the factorial dimen-sionality as well as the factorial similarity in two groups (young and old) [8]. By means of independent factor analyses in the two groups, six pairs of similar attitudinal dimensions emerged. These dimensions cover an "applied" aspect of the perceptions of old age, which has hitherto received little scientific attention [9].

Assuming that there can exist a direct relationship between attitudes toward the elderly's social activities (personal attributes) and perceptions of old people per se (persons), it could in some sense be said that the present approach is concerned with the behavior implications of such an "overlying" attitude. For such a direct relationship to be tenable, we should, with Heider's terms, hypothesize a perceived *unit relation* between the perceived person and his behavior [10]. There are, however, certain theoretical difficulties in assuming that this unit relation prevails. Accordingly, inferences between these two conceptually different attitudinal approaches—e.g., inferences from the present dimensions to attitudes toward old people per se, and conversely—cannot be undertaken in a straightforward fashion. Therefore, it is questionable whether it would be reasonable to generalize the generally negative attitudes—so often reported in US studies—as appropriate for the present ones.

Until recently, research on correlates of perceptions has regularly been limited to zero-order correlations or mean differences. A second limitation has been the populations studied; they have often been selective samples such as (American) college students, which implies severe restrictions upon the generality of the findings. In his review, McTavish emphasized the need for carefully drawn samples from broad sampling frames and a multidimensional approach in mapping out intergenerational perceptions. These two suggestions were particularly relevant to the present study.

The six dimensions now to be examined are assumed to be of social and psychological significance for adults and the elderly alike, though from differ-ent viewpoints. With social integration of the aged as the core tenet, my contention is that perceptions of age-functional behavior may determine the actual behavior and also be antecedents to behavior change; data presented by Neugarten, Moore, and Lowe suggest similar influences from normative expec-tancies on age-appropriate social behavior [11]. Specifically, the present dimensions may be assumed to influence the young and middle-aged's relations with the elderly and also to influence the individual's own development and adjustment to old age [5, 12]. Besides these behavior-influential properties, the attitudes may also be assumed—in virtue of their relationship—to be indicators of self-conception and well-being among the elderly, issues which have formed a gerontological approach yielding significant contributions [13]. Thus, to the extent that, for example, positive attitudes are prevalent among the elderly, it could be inferred that they also are rather well-off in these other respects. It is further generally agreed that attitudes held by others have important influences on age-identification [13].

Considering these general notions about attitudes as important pieces in our puzzle, a close examination of them becomes still more important. More formally, the present study sought to answer the following questions: How are the elderly in Sweden perceived of with respect to the previously-labeled dimensions Work, Social Work, Gatherings, Dwelling, Welfare, and Administratorship? What is the opinion of the general public, as compared with the attitudes of the elderly themselves? Which variables are likely to influence attitudes among people in general and among the elderly? The latter question, being a major objective of the study, was split into two issues:

1. to explore which of various demographical and attitudinal variables tend to be associated with the dimensions, and
2. to determine how influential these correlates were.

Both issues will be considered simultaneously by means of regression techniques. Presumably, the correlates will have different predictive power among the dimensions because the latter refer to diversified aspects of societal relations. It is further suggested that—by analyzing young and old separately—crucial correlates will have a better chance of being discernible, the rest being ignored.

METHOD

Participants

The samples used in the present analysis were two sub-samples from a total of 1303 participants representing a random sample of noninstitutionalized Swedish men and women in six age strata who returned a mailed questionnaire. Approximately the same number of men and women was in each age group, and the response rate in the original sample survey was 88 per cent [14]. Initially, two cooperating research groups focused on attitudes toward:

1. the elderly [15] and
2. retirement and retirees [14].

Their two data sets were later combined into a joint study [8]. By dividing the sample into two groups it was possible to study separately the factorial dimensionality in these two groups, called "Adults" and "Retirees," where both expressed attitudes toward the latter. Thus, the group labeled Retirees coincided with the definition assigned to both attitudinal referent groups, namely, "people aged 70-80 years" [15] and "retirees." [14] (Originally, the term "pensioner" was employed, this being in Sweden an everyday designation for aged people; the Retiree group also included some working participants.)

Except for some shrinkages, the present regression analyses were performed in samples identical with those where the factorial dimensions were studied:

1. The *Adult* sample comprehended 333 nonretired participants aged thirty, forty-five, sixty, and sixty-five, and
2. the *Retirees* were constituted by 243 participants aged seventy and seventy-five.

Due to various questions about work and retirement, several participants had previously been deleted: from Adults and Retirees, respectively, nineteen and seventy-three housewives without work attachment had been discarded, as well as eighteen and twenty-one participants because of missing responses to these questions (which may have been felt irrelevant in some instances). With due reservations for exclusions and drop-outs, the participants can be regarded as representing a random sample of individuals within the specified age cohorts.

The two groups were analyzed separately, primarily because of the conceptually different relations between the respondent groups and the referent group (Adult and Retirees expressed attitudes toward Retirees), and also because of the different phrasing and implications of the variables pertaining to work and retirement.

Attitude Dimensions

As attitude measures were used the six dimensions from the previous factor analysis and for which factorial similarity and internal consistency in the two groups had been demonstrated, thus further admitting a dimension-wise comparison between groups [8].

The four dimensions labeled Social Work, Gatherings, Dwelling, and Administratorship were extracted from items constructed by Annell et al., who directed their interest toward certain activities thought to be of relevance for the elderly [15]. The investigators' referent group was "people aged seventy to eighty years and in a fairly good state of health." The two dimensions entitled Work and Welfare came from items devised by the other project team, which focused on retirement issues and consequently labeled their referent group "retirees." [14] (The items comprised by the dimensions are listed in [8].) More specifically, the dimension Work dealt with possibilities for continued work after retirement; Social Work concerned chiefly guidance work among youngsters in the leisure field; Gatherings comprehended various forms of social intercourse; Dwelling concerned age-integrated/segregated housing for the elderly; Welfare contained statements about the well-being and social welfare of the retirees; and Administratorship dealt with bureaucratic aptitude and contacts with authorities. The order of dimensions is presented according to a higher-order factor analysis, grouping the first three and the next two dimensions into two second-order factors, respectively. Administratorship was grouped along with dimensions not used here.

The Likert-type items used a five-alternative response mode varying from "completely agree" to "completely disagree." The values of +2 and -2 were assigned to the extremes of agreement and disagreement, respectively, and a zero value to represent the midpoint alternative "as much speaks for as against."

Correlates

Six *demographical measures* were used: age, education, sex, occupation, residence, and social position. Education was coded as 1 to 6, where the lowest level corresponds to elementary school and the highest to university studies [15]. Sex was scored 0 and 1 for females and males, respectively. Occupation is equivalent to the customary Swedish trichotomized social class stratification, where occupation is the primary source of classification into high, medium, and low level (here scored 3, 2, and 1, respectively [14]). Residence was dichotomized into rural (0) and urban (1) location on the basis of postal number: As urban citizens were classified those living in the three towns of the county (with more than 7,000 inhabitants). Social position is an additive composite of the five previous measures, scored according to suggestions by Galtung, who developed and investigated an index constructed upon eight dichotomized social-rank variables and found it useful in studying opinions regarding foreign policy [16]. His scale was based upon a theoretical "center-periphery"-dimension of total social rank position. Five of Galtung's eight variables were dichotomized and assigned separate scores of 0 or 1 to each individual. Thus, the present individuals who were assigned zero scores were:

1. aged seventy and seventy-five;
2. low-educated (elementary school);
3. females;
4. rural residents; and/or
5. those classified in the low (1) level of occupation;

otherwise they were given a score of 1 per variable. The index was finally obtained by adding these five scores. For obvious reasons the effect of the age variable is not included in the index as it was used here, because the Adult-Retiree dichotomization was based upon age. Thus, we have a 5-point scale to measure how "centrally" located a person is.

Attitudes toward work and retirement—Because of our strong cultural emphasis on occupational roles I suggested that orientations toward work and retirement would be of such importance as to be influential in the present dimensional context. Therefore, four questions about actual personal experiences and perceptions were exploratively included. With the appropriate verb tenses, the following questions were asked in the two groups:

1. work satisfaction,
2. sense of loss after retirement (i.e., "Will/Do you miss working?"),
3. looking forward to retirement, and
4. planning for retirement.

Each of the first three questions had identical response categories except for a slight change for question (2) in the Adult group. The categories were similar to those used for the factor-analyzed items but without the midpoint response. The fourth question (plans) had three alternatives (yes, partially, no).

Work after retirement—The Retirees also indicated whether they had worked after retirement. This variable seemed interesting because I had deliberated as to whether the presence or absence of work might be an indicator of a somewhat more general outlook on life. (A "yes" answer to the previous five questions is represented as high scores.)

Contact with older persons (those "over seventy")—was also indicated by the participants. Answers could vary from "daily" to "never," within five alternatives scored 5 to 1 [15].

"When aging begins"—The participants also were asked when, in their opinion, a person is old. They could choose from alternatives varying from "before sixty-five" to "after eighty" (scored 1 to 5 [15]). This variable was not included in the regression analyses, but its zero-order correlations will nevertheless be indicated. Inclusion of this variable would have caused a reduction of sample size ($n = 18$), and even worse, a sampling bias, because these participants (who answered "individually," etc.) tend to be less likely to hold stereotypes about older persons [2]. It may, however, be of some interest to see whether negative attitudes, as found by Tuckman and Lorge [2], are associated with a low age reply in the present data.

Statistical Analyses

The group means for the raw scores were tested in the nonreduced samples ($n_A = 370$, $n_R = 337$) by use of two-tailed t tests. (Subscripts A (Adults) and R (Retirees) are used to denote the particular groups.) The means were tested for group differences as well as for determining whether they were significantly different from zero (i.e., the midpoint alternative). The standard deviations for the Adult and Retiree dimensions were in the ranges of 1.0-1.3 and 1.2-1.3, respectively.

Factor scores were estimated jointly for both groups by linear multiple regressions of the dimensions on the variables and were obtained as standard values after oblique rotations according to the BMDX72 program ("direct quartimin"), with squared multiple correlations as communality estimates [17-19]. These scores were used as dependent variables in the regression analyses, which were performed with the program BMDP2R [20]. This program computes multiple linear regression equations in a step-wise manner.

Age, education, and sex, whether significant or not, were forced into the equations, in order to check for the unique variance contribution of these apparently most influential variables among the six demographical ones. The forced-option was chosen because above all these three variables were almost invariably the most powerful single demographical predictors in both groups when stepping with significant increase in the multiple correlation (R) as the only criterion for including new variables. In these nonforced procedures occupation and residence both failed to enter the equations, and social position entered only for $Work_A$ and $Gatherings_R$. In addition, in the Adult sample, age, education, and sex all had significant zero-order correlations with almost all dimensions.

The entry and removal of the rest of the correlates was based upon increasing Rs. Each step was considered significant only if the inclusion of a new variable caused a significant $(p < .05)$ increase in variance [21]. An F test was performed for the zero-order correlations not entering the equations, showing whether they were different from zero.

The t and F tests being rather robust with respect to violations of assumptions, the testing procedures must, however, be regarded as approximate, because the assumptions were not exactly satisfied. Throughout this paper, the conceptual unit for significance levels will be the single comparison.

RESULTS

Dimensions: Group Mean Values

In Table 1 the figures of the first row present the group means for the dimensional raw scores. Values different from zero (assumed to represent a "neutral" attitude) are indicated by asterisks.

For the dimensions Work and Integrated Dwelling there seemed to be an almost complete consensus between Adults and Retirees. Their mean values were not significantly different from the response alternative phrased "by and large agree" $(p > .10)$. Regarding the four other dimensions, however, there was substantial disagreement between the groups. In relative and absolute

Table 1. Attitudinal Dimensions: Means, Partial-Regression Coefficients, Zero-Order Correlations, and Explained Variance

	Dimensions											
	Work		Social Work		Gatherings		Dwelling (Age-Integrated)		Welfare		Admin	
Means, Correlates, Variance	Adult	Ret	Adult	Ret	Adult	Ret	Adult	Ret	Adult	Ret	Adult	Ret
Mean Agreement (370, 337)[a]	99**	92**	15*	-56**	45**	-11	90**	90**	-41**	-06	-05	14
Old Age (321, 237)[a,b]	++	+		++		++	++	+			++	+
Predictors (333, 243)[a]												
Age	-14**	10	-30**	-09	-15**	-03	-15**	06	27**	06	-08	13*
Education	10*	-10	17**	09	12*	22**	21**	04	-36**	-18**	20**	09
Sex	-18**	-24**	-11*	14*	-14**	12	-11*	-10	01	-04	00	14*
Residence											11*	
Occupation	++		++	++	+	++	++		--		++	
Social Position			+			++	++		--	-	++	
Work												
Satisfaction	31**	29**		+		21**	11*	18**				23**
Loss		+										
Retirement												
Anticipation	--	-		-18**	-	--	--					
Planning	14**			+		+			++			
Working R		15*				++						
Contacts		13*		13*		24**						
Variance												
R^2aes	09	05	16	03	07	04	11	02	25	03	06	04
R^2incr	11	15	00	05	00	11	01	03	00	00	01	05
R^2tot	19	20	16	08	07	15	12	06	25	03	07	09

Note: Decimal points omitted. Blanks indicate non-significant values. Signs (+, -) indicate direction of zero-order correlations; number of signs refer to significance level (e.g., ++ means $p < .01$, + means $p < .05$). Males coded as 1, females as 0; urban citizens coded as 1, rural as 0. Asterisks indicate significance levels for means and β weights different from zero.

[a] Numbers in parentheses indicate the number of Adults and Retirees, respectively.
[b] This variable was not used in the regression analyses.
* $p < .05$.
** $p < .01$.

Note:	– means one minus sign;
	– – means two minus signs.

terms, Adults were significantly more positive than Retirees toward Social Work ($p < .001$). There was a similar trend for Gatherings ($p < .001$), except that Retirees tended to be neutral. The Retirees also were neutral toward Welfare, whereas Adults were rather negatively disposed, i.e., they perceived the social welfare for the elderly to be rather low; the group means were significantly different ($p < .001$). For the dimension Administratorship there was a tendency for both groups to be neutral, the Retirees, however, being relatively more favorably inclined ($p < .02$).

When Aging Begins

As the signs (+) for "Old Age" indicate (Table 1), this variable had significant zero-order correlations with three and five dimensions for Adults and Retirees, respectively. Parenthetically, the correlation between this variable and one's own age was negligible (−.02 in both groups). In general, to the extent that negative perceptions were noticeable, they seemed to be associated with a tendency to answer a low age for "when aging begins," especially among Retirees. Similar findings were reported by Tuckman and Lorge [2]. Whatever the reasons, this relation is consistent with our cultural evaluation of youth.

Regression Analyses

In Table 1 are also presented the standardized partial-regression coefficients (β weights) and three variance terms for each dimension and group. Variables in the equations are referred to as "predictors." The significance levels for the final β weights are indicated by means of asterisks. Column-wise, the R^2 coefficients represent the proportion of the total variation in each dimension that can be accounted for by linear regression on the various correlates: The variance term for age, education, and sex (R^2_{aes}) tells how much variance the three forced variables jointly account for; the variance increment term (R^2_{incr}) is a measure of variance attributable to the rest of the variables; and the total attitudinal variance is expressed in R^2_{tot}. Table 1 also summarizes the significant zero-order correlations for variables not entering the equations by means of signs (+ and −), indicating direction and significance level. They can be regarded as indicators of construct validity, but also of how much has been acquired in predictive simplicity by the regression technique.

The least successfully predicted dimensions were Gatherings and Administratorship among Adults, and Welfare among Retirees, whereas the most successful dimension, in terms of the joint Adult and Retiree evidence, seemed to be Work, explained by about 20 per cent of the variance. Curiously enough, Welfare was the best predicted dimension among Adults and the least among Retirees (25 and 3%, respectively).

Demographical variables—Taken together, age, education, and sex accounted for different proportions of variance as seen in the R^2_{aes} row, varying from 2 to 25 per cent for Dwelling$_R$ and Welfare$_A$, respectively. Over all dimensions, age, education, and sex were markedly more influential among Adults. When comparing the relative influence of these three variables with the remaining correlates, the average variances for each dimension among Adults were .12 and .02 and among Retirees .04 and .07, respectively. Within groups, age and education seemed to be relatively more dominant than sex among Adults, and sex, though moderately, the most influential variable of the three among Retirees. For Adults, the following pattern seemed valid for the first five dimensions: Young, well-educated, and females were, in relative terms, more positively inclined and tended also to perceive the elderly as suffering from a lower degree of welfare. A positive perception of Administratorship was significantly related to high education. No such clear pattern was found among Retirees; nor did the weights approach significance to the same extent: The well-educated were positive toward Gatherings and perceived Welfare to be relatively low; females were in favor of Work and males were favorable toward Social Work and Administratorship; and age, the least salient variable, indicated that the elderly retired were relatively in favor of Administratorship.

The fact that both social position and occupation correlated highly with several of the dimensions can be referred to previous attitudinal studies, where it has been demonstrated that the attitudes were influenced by similar variables [4-6]. Nevertheless, in the present study, both these correlates were completely partialled out by one or more of the three forced ones. Residence entered only once (Administratorship$_A$), which indicates that this variable exerted a diminishing influence in this context.

The disappointing predictive ability of the social position index deserves a special comment. In the cases of significant zero-order correlations, the influence of the index regularly was reduced to a nonsignificant partial correlation when education or age entered the equation. Even though social position is a composite of education and sex among the forced variables, "something" should have been left to be explained when these two were partialled out. Hence, we must conclude that education, age, and sex—either separately or jointly—generally were superior predictors in terms of conceptual simplicity as well as the number of their significant figures relative to the nonsignificant zero-order correlations of the social position index.

Work-retirement correlates—As previously indicated, the questions about work and retirement, as well as the contact variable, accounted generally for more variance among Retirees than among Adults (the average variances for each dimension were .07 and .02, respectively).

Work satisfaction did, unexpectedly, not enter into the dimension Work, but was instead clearly related to Dwelling, namely, those Adults and Retirees reporting high work satisfaction tended also to be in favor of Integrated Dwelling, with those Retirees also being favorable toward Administratorship.

The influence of the rest of the correlates seemed, in terms of the β weights, restricted to the first three dimensions (previously factored into a higher-order factor called "Social Activities") [8]. Anticipated and reported loss of work in retirement had strong relationships with Work and Gatherings$_R$.

The extent to which the participants (had) looked forward to retirement ("Anticipation") was initially negatively related to several dimensions, but the zero-order correlations were, except for Social Work$_R$, partialled out. (The magnitude of the correlations among Adults was primarily due to age effects: As soon as age entered the equation, the partial correlations approached zero.)

Planning for retirement entered the equations positively only for Work$_A$, but initially correlated positively also with Social Work and Gatherings among Retirees. Those Retirees reporting that they had worked after retirement were positive toward Work. (There was also a weak relation with Social Work and Gatherings, as the zero-order correlations indicate.)

Contacts—The frequency of contacts with the elderly did not at all influence the dimensions among Adults. On the other hand, those Retirees having more frequent contact tended to be more favorable on the first three dimensions.

DISCUSSION

The results clearly indicate the multifaceted aspects of the dimensions: There are similar as well as different views between Adults and Retirees, and the influences of various correlates are diversified. Although the regression analyses explained only fractional proportions of the attitudinal variance, some significant correlates were distinguished. The results for the Retirees' work and retirement perceptions, for example, suggest that these factors are promising.

Thus, a single, general conclusion about the correlates of these attitudes is not warranted on the basis of the present results. Rather, such statements must be qualified with respect to a certain dimension as well as group.

Three limitations must be mentioned. First, the cross-sectional design confounds developmental and cohort effects [11, 22]. The daily bread for some of us is to restate the problem of age differences thus: To what extent are they accountable for by age per se (i.e., psychological and maturational variables) and to what extent are they due to environmental processes (i.e., generational and cultural effects)? One might ask: Are the younger people's more "positive" perceptions due to our cultural emphasis on activity and efficacy, whereas—when one grows older and faces the problems of being old— another outlook on life and other quality-of-life values become pronounced? Such suggestions *may* account for the present age differences, but the data do not permit definite conclusions.

Second, societal changes over time are likely to affect the attitudes. For example, in times of youth unemployment it is sometimes argued that older workers should retire and "let them take their place" (cf. dimension Work). Therefore, it is unclear to what extent the results depict a contemporary state.

The third limitation is related to validity in the case of Retirees. They were asked to indicate their perceptions of a whole group (Retirees), but it is uncertain to what extent they gave "personal" answers: Some individuals may have had quite different views about the group and the self, and replied in concordance with either of those two referents. Thus, there may be some confusion of attitudes. Another difficulty is that the three questions about work and retirement required recall information. Nevertheless, although the data contained information about perceptions modified by later experiences, they should be valuable and relevant.

The general contention that the societal views of the aged are very much related to the self-views expressed by older persons about themselves received only partial support in terms of the group mean comparisons [13]. In this dimensional context, Adults tended to hold more favorable attitudes than Retirees toward Social Work, Gatherings, and Welfare, and were more negative toward Administratorship. (Adults' negative evaluations of Welfare can in some sense be said to be a positive point of view.) In short, the elderly themselves appeared to subscribe more to negative perceptions than the younger group in these respects. These findings are almost the obverse of those reported in several studies which compared perceptions among young and old individuals [4, 5, 9]. Nevertheless, evidence on this topic is not entirely clearcut, presumably depending upon the diversity of measuremental techniques employed.

Comparisons of correlates among Adults and Retirees delineated some points of difference between the two groups. First, age exerted an almost overwhelming influence among Adults, possibly due to the wider age span (thirty-five years, as opposed to five for Retirees). Second, education was likewise more pronounced among Adults. Third, there was a significant tendency among Adult females to perceive the elderly more positively than did Adult males on the four dimensions Work, Social Work, Gatherings, and Dwelling. Among Retirees, on the other hand, females were positive only toward Work. This indicate a more complex Age × Sex interaction than previously reported, as also shown by McTavish [4] and Weinberger and Millham [7]. Finally, the work-retirement variables were more salient correlates among Retirees than Adults, as was also the frequency of contacts with the elderly. The reason why these same relationships were not evidenced to the same extent among Adults may be possible weak associations between one's own work commitment and the dimensions (these latter referring to other persons). It is not obvious why closeness of contact failed to interfere with the perceptions among Adults; although Drake reported no relation [23], other investigators, mostly studying students' perceptions, have reported a negative relationship between contact and stereotypic attitudes [3-6]. However, the quantitative measurement may have been too simple; the quality and meaning of associational contacts could have been taken into account.

Education deserves an additional note. The tendency for both groups generally was that the well-educated were more favorable. The present findings were in agreement with the uniform tendency reported elsewhere, namely, that the low-educated appear more negative and hold more prejudices toward ethnic and minority groups as well as toward the elderly [24, 25]; however, education does not seem to have been examined in the numerous earlier studies on this topic [4, 5]. Two suggestions seem appropriate in this study:

1. The well-educated may have greater response sophistication, and
2. because the well-educated generally are recruited from privileged social classes, they may also have a more favorable image of old age [24].

Turning to the three dimensions Work, Social Work, and Gatherings as related to the Retirees' work commitment and retirement anticipations, the results indicated that a positive social outlook was partially related to positive work orientations and experiences as well as peer affiliations. It may be speculated whether the work-retirement variables were for Retirees indicative of a desire to re-engage in the work role as well as in other activities, a suggestion consistent with the crisis theory [26]. Including the dimension Integrated Dwelling into this context, where work satisfaction also entered positively, it is suggestive to think about some common core of social engagement versus withdrawal as an underlying bipolar concept. I wonder if "retirement" could be thought of as covering a broader social phenomenon: For the Retirees, to retire is not only a matter of ceasing to work but also a question of withdrawal from other activities, as well. (Though beyond the present scope, personality dimensions such as extroversion-introversion may be invoked here.)

Adults and Retirees were in agreement with each other with respect to the desirability of continued Work and Integrated Dwelling, whereas their preferences were at variance regarding Social Work and Gatherings. To put this another way, let us consider the first two dimensions as related to continued involvement in previous roles and the next two as pertaining to issues demanding new sets of role behaviors (operationally, Social Work and Gatherings comprehended some suggested "new" activities [8]). Viewed this way, the conflicting attitudes can be assumed for the Retirees as being due to resistance to engagement in new social roles ensued, in turn, by persistence of value orientations, namely, prevailing cohort expectations of age-appropriate behavior. On the other hand, the more favorable attitudes of Adults may be accounted for by an open-mindedness toward the suggested activities.

Adults and younger persons held low estimates of the social Welfare for the elderly. It may tentatively be suggested that the sociological explanatory concept of "relative deprivation" is appropriate: The elderly compared themselves with the aged in days of yore; Adults, especially the younger ones—who have a shorter time perspective—viewed the elderly as not sharing their own present rise in standard. The dimension Administratorship—somewhat odd in this dimensional context, emphasizing social relations—was the only instance where the elderly had a more positive appreciation than Adults of the capacity of the Retirees. This finding was consistent with most of the previous American research which compared young and old individuals [4, 5].

Parts of the results can be related to the theoretical disengagement-activity-controversy, although the theories do not explicitly address themselves to *perceptions* of age-functional behavior. In brief, disengagement theory assumes generational mutual withdrawal as a natural freeing process, while activity theory holds that an individual will seek to maintain previous levels of activity [27]. The disengagement contention does not seem supported by the joint Adult and Retiree perceptions when considering Work and Integrated Dwelling: Both groups appear to hold the same positive views. Adding Social Work and Gatherings, however, the picture becomes less clear: While Adults still are positive, Retirees seem reluctant, if not negative. Thus, among Adults there does not appear to be a general expectation of "withdrawal." Nevertheless, conveying the negative views among Retirees as due to the novelty of the activities, these perceptions may have other causes, but can scarcely be explained solely in terms of wishes to withdraw.

CONCLUSIONS

Thus far, the results clearly indicate the multidimensional character of the perceptions of elderly people's social life. Even though methodological and cultural differences as well as time changes prohibit a general explanation for the various American and Swedish findings, the uniformly positive perceptions among Adults may indicate a pronounced social awareness, especially among younger, well-educated, and female ones. The study suggests further that society (i.e., "Adults") approves of and expects interactive behavior from the able elderly. Nevertheless, the perceptions among the elderly themselves seem more differentiated: It is suggested that they approve of continued involvement in previous social roles whereas they seem slightly reluctant to engage in new activities.

REFERENCES

1. J. Tuckman and I. Lorge, Attitudes Toward Old People, *The Journal of Social Psychology, 37,* pp. 249-260, 1953.
2. J. Tuckman and I. Lorge, "When Aging Begins" and Stereotypes About Aging, *Journal of Gerontology, 8,* pp. 489-492, 1953.

3. J. Tuckman and I. Lorge, Attitude Toward Aging of Individuals With Experiences with the Aged, *The Journal of Genetic Psychology, 92,* pp. 199-204, 1958.
4. D. G. McTavish, Perceptions of Old People: A Review of Research Methodologies and Findings, *The Gerontologist, 11:*4, part 2, pp. 90-101, 1971.
5. A. H. Nardi, Person-Perception Research and the Perception of Life-Span Development, *Life-Span Developmental Psychology, Personality and Socialization,* P. B. Baltes and K. W. Schaie (eds.), Academic Press, New York, 1973.
6. P. J. Naus, Some Correlates of Attitudes Towards Old People, *The International Journal of Aging and Human Development, 4,* pp. 229-243, 1973.
7. L. E. Weinberger and J. Millham, A Multi-Dimensional, Multiple Method Analysis of Attitudes Toward the Elderly, *Journal of Gerontology, 30,* pp. 343-348, 1975.
8. J. Skoglund, A Comparative Factor Analysis of Attitudes Toward Societal Relations of the Elderly, *The International Journal of Aging and Human Development, 8,* pp. 277-291, 1977-78.
9. V. Wood, Age-Appropriate Behavior for Older People, *The Gerontologist, 11:*4, part 2, pp. 74-78, 1971.
10. F. Heider, *The Psychology of Interpersonal Relations,* Wiley, New York, chapter 7, 1958.
11. B. L. Neugarten, J. W. Moore and J. C. Lowe, Age Norms, Age Constraints, and Age Socialization, *Middle Age and Aging,* B. L. Neugarten, (ed.), University of Chicago Press, Chicago, 1968.
12. R. Kastenbaum and N. Durkee, Young People View Old Age, *New Thoughts on Old Age,* R. Kastenbaum, (ed.), Springer, New York, 1964.
13. G. R. Peters, Self-Conceptions of the Aged, Age Identification, and Aging, *The Gerontologist, 11:*4, part 2, pp. 69-73, 1971.
14. A. Askelöf and J. Skoglund, (*Fixed Age of Retirement: The Double Compulsion*), unpublished thesis, University of Uppsala, Department of Psychology, 1972.
15. E. Annell, K. Faxér and M. Norman, (*Effects of Various Factors Upon Attitudes Toward People Between 70 and 80*), unpublished thesis, University of Uppsala, Department of Psychology, 1971.
16. J. Galtung, Foreign Policy Opinion as a Function of Social Position, *Journal of Peace Research, 1,* pp. 206-231, 1964.
17. R. I. Jennrich and P. F. Sampson, Rotation for Simple Loadings, *Psychometrika, 31,* pp. 313-323, 1966.
18. W. J. Dixon, (ed.), *BMD. Biomedical Computer Programs. X-Series Supplement,* University of California Press, Berkeley, 1972.
19. R. L. Gorsuch, *Factor Analysis,* Saunders, Philadelphia, chapter 6, 1974.
20. W. J. Dixon, (ed.), *BMDP. Biomedical Computer Programs,* University of California Press, Berkeley, 1971. (Program revised January 29, 1973.)
21. J. E. Overall and C. J. Klett, *Applied Multivariate Analysis,* McGraw-Hill, New York, chapter 17, 1972.
22. K. W. Schaie, Methodological Problems in Descriptive Developmental

Research on Adulthood and Aging, *Life-Span Developmental Psychology. Methodological Issues*, J. R. Nesselroade and H. W. Reese, (eds.), Academic Press, New York, 1973.

23. J. T. Drake, Some Factors Influencing Students' Attitudes Toward Older People, *Social Forces, 35*, pp. 266-271, 1957.

24. J. A. Thorson, Attitudes Toward the Aged as a Function of Race and Social Class, *The Gerontologist, 15:*4, pp. 343-344, 1975.

25. C. Bagley, Prejudice in England, *Attitudes*, N. Warren and M. Jahoda, (eds.), Penguin, Harmondsworth, 2nd ed., 1973.

26. B. D. Bell, The Limitations of Crisis Theory as an Explanatory Mechanisn in Social Gerontology, *The International Journal of Aging and Human Development, 6*, pp. 153-168, 1975.

27. R. J. Havighurst, B. L. Neugarten and S. S. Tobin, Disengagement and Patterns of Aging, *Middle Age and Aging*, B. L. Neugarten, (ed.), University of Chicago Press, Chicago, 1968.

ACKNOWLEDGEMENT

The University of Uppsala provided computer time. Research grants for collecting data were available through the agency of K. Roos, assistant county medical officer in Uppsala. I am gratefully indebted to E. Annell, K. Faxér, and M. Norman for their kindness in providing me with access to their raw data cards, and to my previous coauthor A. Askelöf for his invaluable contributions in the earlier stages of the project. I would also like to thank B. Edvardsson and J. Vegelius for their useful comments on an earlier draft of this paper.

chapter 7

SOME PROBLEMS OF THE AGED IN
THE RURAL MILIEU IN ISRAEL

Yitzchak Berman

INTRODUCTION

Israel is an urbanized country. In 1972, 84.4% of the population lived in urban areas. The Jewish population in Israel, which makes up 85.3% of the population, is even more urbanized, where 90.3% live in urban areas. The non-Jewish population is predominantly rural, and only 49.7% live in urban areas. Israel is the 3rd most urbanized country in the world according to the U.N. Demographical Yearbook, 1970.

While Israel is predominantly an urban nation, the ideology and spirit of the country is rural. The Jewish settlers who came to Palestine from the 1880's onward, escaping from religious persecution, came with a nationalistic, socialistic ideology and manifested this ideology in rural settlement. The pioneers returning to their homeland founded unique types of settlements which were conducive to the economic and social demands of the time. The "Moshav," a rural settlement, organized as a cooperative, where the purchase of agricultural equipment and the marketing of produce are collective, but consumption and most of the production are private, became the predominant way of rural life among the Jews. The "collective Moshav," is a rural settlement where in addition to the cooperative characteristics of the "moshav," the production is collective and only consumption is private, is a recent innovation in rural living. The Kibbutz, the first of which was founded in 1909 on the shores of Lake Kinneret, and which plays an important role in the ideological life of the nation, is a rural settlement where both production and consumption are collective. Table 1

Table 1. Population (thousands) and Locality by Type of Locality and Population Group[a]

	Total	Per cent	1972 Jewish	Per cent	Arab	Per cent
Total	3,232.3 (100)		2,755.5 (85.3)		476.9 (14.7)	
Urban	2,725.7 (84.4)		2,488.6 (90.3)		237.1 (49.7)	
Rural	504.0 (15.8)	100.0	264.2	100.0	279.8 (50.3)	100.0
Villages	216.9	49.0	23.9	9.0	193.1	80.5
Moshavim (including Collective Moshavim)	134.4	26.7	124.0	50.7	.4	0.2
Kibbutzim	90.0	17.8	89.8	34.0	.2	0.1
Temporary Settlements and Bedouin Tribes	44.0	8.7	—		44.0	18.3
Institutions and Farms	14.6	2.9	14.4	5.4	.1	—
Living Outside Settlements	4.1	.9	2.1	0.9	2.0	0.9

[a] Statistical Abstract of Israel AB No. 24, Central Bureau of Statistics, Jerusalem.

shows the distribution of the Jewish population in these rural settlements.

The non-Jewish population is more rural than the Jewish population, and live predominantly in village-type settlements (40.5%) where production, consumption, purchase, and sales are generally on a private base.

THE AGED IN RURAL AREAS

In 1972, 7.4% of the Jewish population was over the age of 65. Only 3.6% of the non-Jewish population was in this age-group. Through a special analysis of the population lists of the Ministry of the Interior data on the aged by locality was obtained. Only 10.1% of all the aged in Israel lived in rural areas. 93.2% of all the Jewish aged lived in urban areas and only 6.8% or 14,829 Jewish aged, lived in rural areas. The Jewish aged population lived in three main types of settlements: 2,936 (19.8%) lived in villages; 6,841 (46.1%) lived in Moshavim; and 4,065 (27.4%) lived in Kibbutzim (see Table 2).

52.4% of all the non-Jewish aged lived in urban areas and 47.6 per cent or 8,878 non-Jewish aged lived in rural areas. 86.7% or 7,702 of all the non-Jewish aged lived in villages (see Table 2).

Table 2. Population of Aged (65+) by Locality
and Population Group

Locality	Jews		Non Jews	
	No.	Per cent	No.	Per cent
Total	217,453		18,659	
Urban	202,624 (93.2)		9,781 (52.4)	
Rural	14,829 (6.8)	100	8,878 (47.6)	100
Villages	2,936	19.8	7,702	86.7
Moshavim	6,841	46.1	—	
Kibbutzim	4,065	27.4	—	
Bedouin Tribes	—		1,076	12.1
Other	987	6.7	100	1.2

THE PROBLEMS OF THE AGED

As the types of rural settlements are very different from one another, in order to understand the problems of the aged in rural areas one must analyze the problems according to type of settlement and only after such an analysis may one come to general conclusions of the problems of the aged in rural areas.

The Moshav

"Moshavim" may be divided into two main types based on the year the "Moshav" was founded. These are the veteran Moshavim which were founded before 1948 by Europeans who worked together to establish a strong agricultural base in the new land and whose founders played an important role in the ideological and political life of the new nation. The aged population of this type of Moshav numbered, in 1973, only 2,901 or 42.4% of the total aged moshav population. As the aged in this type of Moshav are mainly well established and manifest few problems we will not include them in our discussion.

The second type of Moshav, the "new Moshav," founded after 1948, made up the main part of the Moshav population. This includes 3,707 aged over the age of 65 which is 57.6% of the total aged Jewish population in Moshav settlements.

The population in this type of Moshav came from Oriental countries where they lived in traditional type family system. There, immigration to Israel was a result not only of choice but also out of hostility of the population of the host country. These Jews came in large numbers after the establishment of the State of Israel to a strange land which was Western oriented and not financially prepared to accept them in large numbers. The result of which was that many Jews were placed in Moshavim with only a minimum of necessities and with no training. The elderly who settled were not at all prepared to live in such a setting. It is these rural settlements which have developed the least and where the most social and economic problems exist. In a study of the aged in these settlements four main problems were found to exist: a) housing, b) income, c) health, and d) social.

Housing. The standard of housing among the aged is of the poorest quality. In many areas the toilet facilities are outside the house. In the home where children are present the aged feel that they live in crowded conditions. Where the aged live alone they live in housing of a lower standard than their children. Heating and hot water were also absent during the winter months.

Though there is a low standard of housing among the aged, most of the elderly (80%) refused to change their housing. This attitude exists as a result of the following two factors:

1. The possibility of moving is remote.
2. The elderly see their home as theirs and fear moving to a strange new place.

Income. The elderly population is not related to the agricultural economy which is the main income activity on the Moshav. Even those elderly who still own their own land do not work it. About 65% of the elderly do not work at all.

The main income source of the elderly is from government sources or from their children. Their income is not stable, with those with better health and education having a higher income.

Health. Health services reach all the aged in these rural settlements when these services are demanded by the aged. Over 95% are covered by health insurance. A special problem arises where the elderly person is not aware of his health condition and therefore does not come in contact with a doctor or nurse thereby increasing the chances of a deterioration of health.

Social. The most significant social group on the Moshav is the family group. It is with this group that the elderly have most of their contact.

The Moshav serves no role whatsoever in the social life of the aged. There are no cultural or social activities for the aged person nor does he have any friends on the moshav. The elderly person does not turn to the institution of the Moshav for help in time of need, nor does he fulfill any public role in the Moshav.

The House of Prayer, the Synagogue, is the main communal institution where the elderly play a role and it is in this setting that the elderly meet each other and other people.

Most of the elderly are passive and find that they do not have any activities to participate in nor any settings where such activities can take place.

Summary. The aged in the new Moshav are economically dependent on others, live in substandard housing, and are socially isolated outside the family setting. It is only in the area of health services that the aged have a standard which is equal to other parts of the population.

Kibbutz

The aged on the kibbutz which make up 27.4% of the total rural aged population manifest different problems than those found in the Moshav.

The elderly on the kibbutz are in an ambivalent position in a future-oriented and youth-oriented society. As hard physical labor is glorified and the farmer-figure is idealized the elderly person who cannot fulfill the role feels left out. Not only is fulfilling a productive role in the Kibbutz important but, as social status in a collective is a function of ability, there is a loss of status on the part of the elderly person. There is an absence of generally accepted norms of retirement; no clear definition of age of retirement or right to progressive reduction of work hours exists and therefore those who cannot work in physical labor full time feel guilty when they must cut their hours short. As a result of the increase in the number of the elderly on the kibbutzim there is a growing need to increase suitable employment opportunities for this group, and when such opportunities come about there is a need to overcome the problem of adaptation to the new job.

As opposed to the Moshav the Kibbutz sees a definite responsibility in overcoming the problems of their aged population. The Kibbutz itself takes on this responsibility seeking very little outside help.

The second generation of youth is called on to continue the values of the founders of the Kibbutz. There is a growing importance of the parent-child relationship in the process of aging. Retirement from work is gradual, part-time workers transferring to lighter tasks. The collectives are developing flexible standards relating to retirement. Gradual retirement spares the elderly worker the shock of an abrupt and total loss of his major social functions. The elderly play a greater role on committees of the Kibbutz, in temporary terms of office in the Kibbutz federation, and in other organizations. There has been a reorganization of work branches in the Kibbutzim and many Kibbutzim have developed light industries and crafts which employ the aging members. There are refresher and retraining seminars for such elderly people.

Villages

The migration balance in all rural settlements is negative with the overwhelming majority of those who left the rural areas being the young. Nowhere is this more manifest than in the non-Jewish villages where the break with the village has been both psychological and physical.

Since 1967 with the growing employment opportunities in the cities the Arab youth have left the villages in even larger numbers. The effect that this exodus has had on the elderly has been traumatic. The elderly who rule the village and the traditional extended family have found their authority being challenged. With their children leaving them and not being dependent on them economically, the traditional family structure in the village has begun to fall apart.

The effect on the elderly has been manifested in many ways. The youth have left the economic and family unit finding better employment elsewhere leaving the family farm to the elderly and those sons who have not left the village. This causes a certain amount of doubt as to the ability of the father to continue the farm as a viable economic unit.

Traditional customs are being challenged, hurting the status of the elderly father in the eyes of the other family members, and with the youth becoming more financially independent, being elderly as a status symbol in general is being challenged.

The percentage of elderly in the villages has not noticeably risen as the youth still consider the village home and return there on vacations. The return of the youth and the clash of values which follows presents a most serious social problem.

SUMMARY

The problems of the aged in the rural milieu are manifested in different types of settlements in different ways, but certain general problems exist.

The social problems are recognized in all types of rural settlements. The elderly find their previous social status being challenged, either by their inability to remain a viable economic producer or by the norms and values of the dominant culture challenging their existing beliefs.

The social problems are related intimately with the economic conditions of the elderly, since economic status is directly related to social status, in various types of settlements in different ways. On the Moshav the aged cannot work their land and are dependent on their children and others for support. On the Kibbutz the elderly cannot work in the status giving physical way which is reserved for the young. In the village the new found affluence of the young challenges the rule of their elders. In all three societies the aged give way to the young.

In only one type of society do we find the elderly being isolated and that is in the Moshav where the aged do not have social status, thereby not holding a functional role in the family unit, a situation which the village elderly have not as yet faced but which is of imminent importance. On the Kibbutz the communal character of the society integrates the aged into the activities of the society.

REFERENCES

Bar Chaim Avrad, Ben Zimra Z. *A Survey to Identify Problems of the Aged in a Rural Area.* The Israel Association for the Advancement of Community and Social Work, November 1970.

Central Bureau of Statistics. *Statistical Abstract of Israel 1973.* Jerusalem, 1973, No. 24.

Nizan, A. *The Living Conditions of the Aged in Israel.* National Insurance Institute, 1963.

Schachar, Shmuel. *The Problems of the Aged in the Kibbutz Movement.* Published by the Confederation of Kibbutz Movements, 1968.

Talmon, Yonina. Aging in Israel, A planned society. *The American Journal of Sociology,* November 1961, Vol. 67, No. 3.

part three

ETHNICITY IN THE U.S.

chapter 8

GENERATION AND
ETHNIC IDENTITY:
A TYPOLOGICAL ANALYSIS*

Robert C. Pierce
Margaret Clark
Sharon Kaufman[1]

As part of a study of the problems of immigrants aging in a culture into which they were not born, we attempted to measure the degree to which families and individuals in three-generational samples from two ethnic communities retain traditional ways of life in an urban American setting. One facet of the relationship of culture to aging is that of "acculturation." Central questions are: How,

*This research was conducted under a grant from the National Institute of Child Health and Human Development (HD 05941, Study II: Ethnic Identity and Adult Development). We wish to acknowledge this support.
[1] Margaret Clark is the principal investigator of the research project of which this analysis is a part. Robert C. Pierce conceived and executed the analysis reported here. Sharon Kaufman compiled the bibliography and assisted in the preparation of the manuscript.

why, and to what extent do immigrants retain their cultural traditions, and how does this retention aid or hinder their adaptation to old age? This report describes the quantitative measures used to construct a typology; the types are further analyzed and discussed separately [1].

Rather than viewing acculturation as a characteristic validly expressed by a single unilinear scale, we have conceived a discrete *types* of acculturation. We have postulated that there might be a "skin-deep" type of acculturation, in which Anglo-American norms, language, and even details of behavior have been learned through cognitive processes—but underlying identity and values may be those of the traditional society. Again, certain individuals with a broad potential for empathy and role-playing might be able to develop a fairly strong identification with both cultures, becoming truly bicultural in some sense. Prestige within the ethnic community, sex-role expectations, or purely economic considerations might be motivational bases for different kinds of acculturation.

Selecting the Dimensions

Following this multi-dimensional model of acculturation, we looked at cognitive, behavioral, and philosophical (or value-orientational) aspects of cultural identification in individuals in Mexican-American and Japanese-American families in San Francisco. Table 1 summarizes some of the characteristics of the sample. With the exception of one individual among the third generation Mexican-Americans, the parents of all of the respondents were of unmixed ethnicity. Although we attempted to obtain respondents distributed evenly among generations, ethnicity, and gender, this proved to be impossible. (The research design for the larger research, of which the present sample is a subset, called for three generations from a single family to be interviewed. As might be imagined, it is extremely difficult to find three family members of different generations who are willing to be interviewed. As a matter of fact, the design strained our resources somewhat past their limit, and we ultimately had some two-generation families and an occasional one-generation unit. The

Table 1. Some Characteristics of the Sample.

	Mexican American			Japanese American		
	1st Gen.	2nd Gen.	3rd Gen.	1st Gen.	2nd Gen.	3rd Gen.
Men	2	2	6	1	2	2
Women	4	8	5	4	4	9
Mean Age	67.2	43.4	21.7	80.6	52.0	23.0
Median Educ.	4 yrs.	7 yrs.	Some college	11 yrs.	12 yrs.	Some college

present sample is approximately half of the size of the sample studied because of missing data on variables crucial to the construction of the typology.)

COGNITIVE SHPERE: ACCULTURATIVE BALANCE SCALE

Our measure of relative knowledge of Anglo and traditional cultures is described in detail elsewhere [2]. Briefly, Acculturative Balance Scale (ABS) scores are based on the number of correctly identified pictures of common Anglo cultural items in relation to the number of correctly identified pictures relating to the respondent's traditional culture. The scores are constructed to that each respondent's score reflects his acculturative balance in comparison with other respondents in his own subculture. Although separate standardization of the two groups precludes direct comparison (of the order, for example, that Mexican Americans are more "acculturated" than Japanese Americans), one can determine whether a subgroup from one ethnic background is comparable to the equivalent subgroup of the other ethnic background. For example, one can say whether the third generation respondents from one group are, relative to their own group, more or less acculturated than the third generation from the other group. To very briefly recapitulate the results presented in Pierce et al. [2], there were substantial differences among generations in both Japanese-American and Mexican-American groups. Not unexpectedly, younger generations showed much greater cognitive acculturation than immigrants. The ABS scores were unrelated to age and to education when the influence of generation was removed.

BEHAVIORAL SPHERE: ETHNICITY

On the basis of previous work [3], a series of questions about social relationships and the level of participation within the respondent's own ethnic group and within the larger community were developed. A substantial portion of the interview guide was designed to elicit information on ethnic behavior and attitudes.

Table 2. Ethnicity Variables

1. Holiday ratio
2. Literacy ratio
3. Fluency ratio
4. Nationality
5. Religion
6. Percent foreign language movies seen
7. Percent traditional Mexican or Japanese foods preferred
8. Proportion of similar background friends
9. Ethnic identification rating
10. Attitude toward own group

Utilizing this interview material, we constructed ten variables that we were willing to accept on theoretical grounds as provisional definers of ethnicity. These ten variables are summarized in Table 2. Since many of these variables have been constructed from two or more interview questions, some explanation is required.

Holiday ratio (Var. 1) was based on questions asked of each respondent regarding holidays which he or she celebrated. We inquired about six Mexican holidays of the Mexican-American respondents; Japanese-American respondents were asked about ten Japanese holidays; and both groups were asked about their celebration of six Anglo-American holidays. Since a different number of traditional holidays are customarily observed in each group, and also since some of the Anglo-American holidays are celebrated in Mexico as well (Easter, for example), statistical adjustments were necessary to obtain comparable scores for the two groups. The adjustments were as follows: for the Japanese-American respondents, the number of currently celebrated Anglo-American holidays was multiplied by 1.67. For the Mexican-American respondents the number of Anglo-American holidays was multiplied by 2.5 and the number of Mexican holidays multiplied by 1.67. This places all holidays for both samples on a scale running from 0 to 10. A "holiday ratio" was then computed:

Holiday ratio = adjusted traditional/(adjusted Anglo + adjusted traditional).

Literacy and fluency ratios (Vars. 2 and 3) were based on ratings made by the interview regarding verbal fluency and reading ability in both English and the respondent's traditional language. These ratings were based partly on the language selected by the respondent for the interview and partly on questions about what kinds of radio and television programs were selected and what kinds of periodicals were read. The ratios were calculated by the following formulae:

Fluency ratio = English fluency/(English fluency + foreign fluency) and

Literacy ratio = English literacy/(English literacy + foreign literacy). Nationality (Var. 4), religion (Var. 5), per cent foreign-language movies seen (Var. 6), per cent traditional Mexican or Japanese foods named as favorites (Var. 7) and proportion of friends with similar ethnic background (Var. 8) are based on the interview data.

The ninth variable, which we have named "Ethnic Identification" was a rating on a five-point scale, with anchor points at one: Weak identification (status as a minority group member seems to be a minimal importance); three: Moderate (ethnic status frankly influences respondent's life); and five: Very strong ethnic identification (much of respondent's psychological energy is directed by minority group status or cultural heritage). Ratings of two and four are intermediate. Individual ratings were made by a psychologist and were based on a review of the entire interview.

The "attitude toward own group" rating (Var. 10) was similarly developed on a five-point scale, ranging from "strongly negative toward own ethnic group" through neutral to "strongly positive toward own ethnic group." This rating, too, was based on the entire interview.

In the cluster analysis described below, generation (first or immigrant, second, and third) and ethnic group membership (Mexican American or Japanese American) were included as variables to see whether these characteristics were related to the ethnic behavior variables described above.

In order to identify dimensions of ethnic behavior, variables were submitted to cluster analysis [4]. The variables of ethnic group membership and generation were suppressed during factoring and reactivated later to examine their relationships to the cluster structure. Our consideration was that they would be related to ethnic behavior, but should not be allowed to define it. Factoring was continued until ninty-two per cent of the communality was exhausted. Iteration was arbitrarily stopped after the fourth iteration if communalities had not converged with a difference of less than .01. On each dimension, the first or "pivot" variable, was selected as the one with the highest variance of squared correlations. (After the first dimension, the pivot variable was the one with the highest variance of squared residual correlations.) Additional variables were selected on the basis of highest mutual colinearity.

Four dimensions emerged from the analysis. Two of these seemed reasonable, but two others seemed unacceptably weak. However, a virtue of Tryon's system of cluster analysis is that one is not committed to a poor solution; one can re-run the analysis, retaining the dimensions or variables which seem to be informative and deleting those which are confusing or too specific. The results of such a "preset" analysis are shown in Table 3. The preset analysis, while only slightly different from the empirical analysis, does seem to be an improvement upon it. The main analytic difference is that the initial communalities were estimated differently—highest absolute r in the empirical analysis, Tryon's "modified approximation B" [4, p. 285] in the preset analysis. Furthermore, in the preset analysis, the first dimension included more variables. Religion: Catholic; Ethnic group membership: Japanese American; and Ethnic group membership: Mexican American; also appeared in this cluster. The second dimension remained the same.

The first dimension we have called *Anglo Face*, as it seems to indicate an outward behavioral adoption of Anglo culture. The second dimension, named *Traditional Orientation*, includes characteristics that do not emulate the American model, but rather reflect the traditional pattern. We will return to these dimensions in Section B below.

PHILOSOPHICAL SPHERE: VALUE ORIENTATIONS

Our original intention was to include the domain of values in the investigation of acculturation types. The instrument selected—the Kluckhohn and Strodtbeck values schedule [5]—had to be revised somewhat for an urban sample, and, for

Table 3. Results of the Preset Cluster Analysis

	Variable	Oblique coefficient
Dimension 1		
(D)	Nationality: U.S.	.71
(D)	Literacy Ratio	.85
(D)	Fluency Ratio	.81
	Generation: Third	.70
	Generation: First	−.69
	Religion: Catholic	−.50
	Ethnic Group Membership: Japanese American	.47
	Ethnic Group Membership: Mexican American	−.47
Dimension 2		
(D)	Attitude toward own group	.88
(D)	Identification Rating	.69
(D)	Percent foreign language movies attended	.54

ease of administration, we did not ask our subjects to make rankings of values but rather simply to select the preferred alternative.

The revised form of the values schedule is composed of seventeen three-alternative items divided into four orientation categories: Activity, Time, Man-nature, and Relational. The Activity category subsumes five questions and the remaining three categories subsume four questions each. Each question has three alternatives which are presumed to tap the three variations of value orientation within each area. Summary scores for each of the twelve variations were constructed by counting the number of times the respondent chose the alternative relevant to each variation.

Two-way analyses of variance, corrected for non-orthogonality of cell frequencies [6] were computed on each of the variation summary scores with ethnic group membership and generation as classifying variables. The results are summarized in Table 5. Out of the twenty-four main effects tested, eight reached significance at the .05 level or better. None of the interactions was significant.

Table 5 presents a closer look at the significant main effects. There are significant ethnic group differences in *becoming, harmony with nature, subjugation to nature*, and *collateral* variations: The Japanese Americans indicate more orientation towards the *becoming, harmony with nature*, and *collateral* variations than do the Mexican Americans; the Mexican Americans indicate a stronger *subjugation to nature* orientation than do the Japanese Americans. There are no ethnic group differences in *time* orientation.

Table 4. Summary of Significant Value Orientation Effects
(Empty cells indicate non-significant effects.)

	Ethnic Group Membership	Generation
Activity		
Being		
Doing		
Being-in-becoming	p < .025	
Time		
Past	p < .025	
Present		p < .05
Future		
Man-Nature		
With	p < .025	
Over	p < .025	
Subjugation	p < .025	
Relational		
Individual		
Collateral	p < .01	p < .025
Lineal		

There are significant generational differences in the *time* orientation: younger generations become increasingly more *present*-oriented and decreasingly past-oriented. There are no significant differences in the *future* variation. Younger generations indicate increasing orientation toward *mastery over nature.*

In order to see whether the values data might be a fruitful addition to a typological analysis, a preliminary attempt to extract a typology from those data alone was made. Our reasoning was that if value types exist, they might form more discrete types in conjunction with other variables. Contrariwise, if individuals are uniformly distributed in the values score space (or twelve dimensions) then the values data cannot contribute to an emerging typology. Unfortunately for our analytic plans, the latter proved to be the case. Scores on each variation were dichotomized as close to the median as possible and the resulting dichotomy patterns were examined to see whether groups of individuals had identical or similar patterns. The thirty-eight respondents available for analysis yielded thirty-six distinct patterns. Since dichotomizing had already condensed scores, it was clear that the patterns of value orientation or our respondents were largely unique. Therefore, the values schedule did not contribute to construction of an ethnic identity typology. We are led to conclude that contact between urban immigrant cultures and the host culture generates complexities in the area of values that are not being tapped by this measurement. On this basis, then, the values orientation data were omitted from the subsequent typological analysis.

Table 5. Means for Significant Main Effects of Variation Summary Scores
(Empty cells indicate non-significant effects.)

| | Ethnic Group Membership | | Generation | | |
	Mexican American	Japanese American	First	Second	Third
Activity (5 items)					
Becoming	1.97	2.80			
Time (4 items)					
Past			.74	.13	.20
Present			1.57	2.40	2.50
Man-Nature (4 items)					
With	.70	1.56			
Over			.96	2.31	1.56
Subjugation	1.57	1.00			
Relational (4 items)					
Collateral	.97	1.64	.87	1.29	1.83

Constructing the Typology

Our next analytic goal was to see whether we could construct ethnic identity types from the data described above. To that end, *ABS, Anglo Face,* and *Traditional Orientation* were used as the basis of a typological analysis.

Simple sum cluster scores, standardized to a mean of 50 and a standard deviation of 10, were obtained; the three-dimensional distance of each respondent from every other respondent was calculated and the distances transformed to correlation coefficients; and the resulting matrix was submitted to OTYPE analysis.[2]

Six types were extracted. Most of the types are fairly "tight," as indicated by the small standard deviations of each composite within the types. The calculated homogeneities [4] are large, ranging between .83 and .96, which indicates that scores within each types are highly similar.

Some of the characteristics of these six types are summarized in Table 6. Profiles for the types are portrayed in Figure 1.

As shown in Table 6, the types are related to generation but not to ethnic group membership. The first two types are almost entirely first generation (8 out of 9 respondents); the second two types are almost entirely second generation (13 out of 15); and the third two types are largely third generation

[2] OTYPE is described in detail in Tryon and Bailey (1970). Briefly the method attempts to identify types by first selecting an arbitrary set of trial "types," assigning each individual to one of the trial types, computing the coordinates of the centroids of the types, and reassigning individuals to the types they are closest to. The process is iterated until the movement of individuals become negligible.

Table 6. Some Characteristics of Ethnic Identity Types

| | Frequency | | | | | | Mean | |
| | Generation | | | Ethnic Group | | | Composite Score | |
Type	1	2	3	MA	JA	ABS	Traditional Orientation	Anglo Face
1	4	0	0	3	1	31.5	34.9	51.1
2	4	1	0	2	3	34.6	47.2	52.6
3	1	5	0	5	1	45.8	48.0	57.4
4	1	8	0	4	5	50.0	50.3	45.3
5	1[a]	0	6	4	3	54.8	54.7	35.5
6	1[a]	2	15	4	6	58.4	57.6	55.1

[a]Foreign-born, but in the G-3 age range.

(21 out of 25). The proportion of each ethnic group within each type was tested against the overall proportion of respondents in each ethnic group; none of the types had a proportion significantly different from the overall proportion, indicating that respondents from each subcultural group are distributed about evenly across the ethnic identity types. From another perspective, each of these types is composed of respondents from different ethnic backgrounds but similar generations.

The differences between the two types within each generation are interesting in themselves. The differences between Type 1 and Type 2, both first generation, are mainly in Traditional Orientation; scores on Acculturative Balance and Anglo Face are about the same for the two types. The difference between Type 3 and Type 4 are mainly in Anglo Face; the other scores are less than a standard deviation apart from type to type. The difference between Type 5 and Type 6 is also basically in Anglo Face. Thus in distinguishing among first generation respondents, Traditional Orientation is the salient dimension. Immigrants appear either to retain their orientation to their original culture or to discard it. At the same time, and more or less independently, they acquire some characteristics of the host culture. Not surprisingly, they have a better

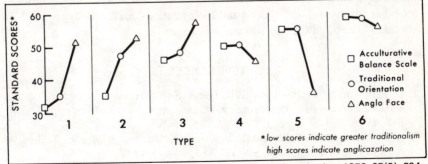

Reproduced from *Human Organization*, 1976, 35(3), 234.

Figure 1.

cognitive grasp of traditional culture than their descendents, and they also have a better cognitive grasp of the original culture than of their adopted culture.

For individuals born in the United States, on the other hand, the salient dimension is Anglo Face. Individuals differ widely on the degree to which they are in sympathy with their parents' or grandparents' culture, and in fact the range of difference seems to grow with generation.

It is also of some interest to note that while Acculturative Balance and Traditional Orientation change substantially from generation to generation, Anglo Face changes little. The implication is that while second and third generation individuals differ appreciably in Anglo Face, they tend to fall into groups which are either high or low on this dimension.

In conclusion, the results of the cluster analysis demonstrated that acculturation can be analyzed into at least two components; had more items been included, and had the domain of values been suitably measured, further dimensions of acculturation may have appeared. Such an investigation ought to be undertaken. The typological analysis demonstrates that Traditional Orientation, Anglo Face, and Acculturative Balance are useful dimensions in describing differences between generations and also for describing differences within generations. Taken together, this analysis indicates that styles of adaptation to a new host culture are not determined solely by age and generation, although these are clearly important factors, but also by personal factors. While these findings constitute no great surprise, we believe that it will prove scientifically useful to construct an empirical foundation for what might otherwise be speculation. Some of the personal factors associated with the acculturation types are discussed in another paper [2].

Pursuit of the line of inquiry suggested by the present research would involve refinement of the measures of the dimensions uncovered. Anglo Face, in particular, needs to be expanded greatly. Composed of only three variables, we cannot claim to have done more than barely identify the dimension. Traditional Orientation would also benefit by the addition of more variables. The Acculturative Balance Scale, we feel, is a substantial measure; but of course it should be cross-validated, and for maximum usefulness should include subscales for other cultures. These factors and their relationships to the types are discussed in detail in Clark, Kaufman, and Pierce [2].

REFERENCES

1. M. M. Clark, S. Kaufman and R. C. Pierce, Explorations of Acculturation: Toward a Model of Ethnic Identity, *Human Organization 35:3*, pp. 231-238, Fall, 1976.
2. R. C. Pierce, M. M. Clark and C. W. Kiefer, A "Bootstrap" Scaling Technique, *Human Organization, 34:4*, pp. 403-410, Winter, 1972.

3. M. M. Clark and B. Anderson, *Culture and Aging,* C. C. Thomas, Springfield, Ill., 1967.
4. R. C. Tryon and D. E. Bailey, *Cluster Analysis,* McGraw Hill, New York, 1970.
5. F. R. Kluckhohn and F. L. Strodtbeck, *Variations in Value Orientations,* Row, Peterson and Co., Evanston, Ill., 1961.
6. B. J. Winer, *Statistical Principles in Experimental Design,* (2nd Ed.) McGraw Hill, New York, 1962.

chapter 9

COGNITIVE ABILITIES: USE OF FAMILY DATA AS A CONTROL TO ASSESS SEX AND AGE DIFFERENCES IN TWO ETHNIC GROUPS*

J.R. Wilson
J.C. DeFries
G.E. McClearn
S.G. Vandenberg
R.C. Johnson
M.N. Rashad

The problem of selective attrition in developmental studies has been clearly identified by Schaie [1]. In effect, the non-random loss of participants in a longitudinal design, or differential non-representativeness of cross-sectional samples, makes it impossible to distinguish between genuine developmental processes and sampling bias.

A partial solution to this problem can be provided in the case of cross-sectional designs when two groups being compared are composed of parents

* The results reported here are made possible by collaboration of a group of investigators (G. C. Ashton, R. C. Johnson, M. P. Mi, and M. N. Rashad at the University of Hawaii, and J. C. DeFries, G. E. McClearn, S. G. Vandenberg, and J. R. Wilson at the University of Colorado) supported by NSF grant GB 34720 and grant MH 06669 from the National Institute of Child Health and Human Development.

and offspring. Under these circumstances, the scores from one generation constitute an expected value for the other generation at that age. For example, data from an offspring can provide an estimate of the performance that would have been characteristic of the parent at that younger age. The precision of the estimate provided in this way is a positive function of the heritability of the trait under investigation. To the extent that environmental factors not common to family members influence the trait, the precision will be reduced. Precision will increase as the number of offspring per parent for whom data are available increases. However, even with relatively low heritability and with few children per parent, useful population trends may be derived if the sample size is sufficiently large.

This report presents age trends for some cognitive ability factors and for some specific cognitive tests. These data were collected as part of a large-scale family study being conducted in Hawaii which has as a primary objective the assessment of genetic and environmental bases of performance on various tests of cognitive ability. Although data collection is still proceeding, the age trends seem sufficiently stable to report at this time.

Since these data were collected at a single point in each individual's life, the comparisons shown are basically cross-sectional in nature. On the other hand, these results include the genetic control mentioned above. The genetic factors involved in the development of cognitive abilities are shared by the older (parental) group and the younger (offspring) group. The genes carried by the offspring are the same ones carried by their parents (barring mutations); therefore, on genetic grounds, mean test or factor scores for the offspring should be similar to the mean test or factor scores for the parents. This is a strong control, as the evidence is overwhelming that within-group heritabilities for some cognitive traits are quite high—on the order of .50 [2] to .80 [3] — so a good proportion of the expected phenotypic variance can thus be minimized or controlled. If we consider the environmental effects as deviations around the expected (or genetic) score with a mean of zero, then the expected test or factor scores for the parents as a group would differ from expected test or factor scores of their offspring only as a function of age differences. This would be an overly simple model, however. It remains entirely possible and reasonable that observed differences represent cohort differences as well. Our parental cohorts had different educational and social experiences from those in the offspring cohort, and the effects of these differences cannot be disentangled from developmental effects on the basis of the present data. Re-testing the younger group several years hence would probably yield a valuable estimate of the cohort effect.

The purposes of the present report are therefore fourfold:

1. to present cross-sectional age curves for the specific tests employed in a large-scale family study in Hawaii;

2. to present cross-sectional age curves for the factors derived from these tests;
3. to examine these age trends by sex and ethnic group; and
4. to introduce a method of genetic control in cross-sectional studies.

Method

PARTICIPANTS

Data obtained from members of 997 families (3268 individuals) will be presented in this report. A family includes both biological parents, 60 years of age or younger, and one or more of their offspring, 14 years of age or older. Families were solicited in a number of ways—including by letter, by radio and television announcements, by contacting clubs and organizations, and, most successfully of all, by personal referral from previous participants. A check for $50 was given to each family immediately after they completed all test procedures.

TESTS

The following tests were administered in the indicated order. Also shown are test times allowed and estimated reliabilities (PUBL = from test manual; KR-20 = Kuder-Richardson Formula 20; CRα = Composite Reliability Coefficient α [4, 5]).

1. Primary Mental Abilities (PMA) Vocabulary, 3 minutes, 0.96 (PUBL)
2. Visual Memory, 1 minute exposure and 1 minute recall, 0.58 (KR-20)
3. Things (a fluency test), 2 parts, 3 minutes each, 0.74 (CRα)
4. Sheppard-Metzler Mental Rotations (modified for group testing by Vandenberg), 10 minutes, 0.88 (KR-20)
5. Subtraction and Multiplication, 2 parts, 2 minutes each, 0.96 (CRα)
6. Elithorn Mazes ("lines and dots"), shortened form, 5 minutes, 0.89 (PUBL)
7. Educational Testing Service (ETS) Word Beginnings and Endings, 2 parts, 3 minutes each, 0.71 (CRα)
8. ETS Card Rotations, 2 parts, 3 minutes each, 0.88 (CRα)
9. Visual Memory (delayed recall), 1 minute, 0.62 (KR-20)
10. PMA Pedigrees (a reasoning test), 4 minutes, 0.72 (PUBL)
11. ETS Hidden Patterns, 2 parts, 2 minutes each, 0.92 (CRα)
12. Paper Form Board, 3 minutes, 0.84 (KR-20)
13. ETS Number Comparisons, 2 parts, 1.5 minutes each, 0.81 (CRα)
14. Whiteman Test of Social Perception, 10 minutes, 0.69 (KR-20)
15. Raven's Progressive Matrices, modified form, 20 minutes, 0.86 (KR-20)

These particular tests were selected on the basis of a pilot study described in detail elsewhere [6]. All tests and a personal history questionnaire were reproduced and bound into a test booklet for use by each subject. The various tests were printed on different colored paper to facilitate monitoring of time limits and of each individual's performance on practice problems.

PROCEDURES

As families reported to the designated testing site they signed a statement indicating their willingness to participate in the research project (including donation of blood and saliva samples), and each individual received a set of gummed labels pre-printed with his code number. All tests and samples were identified only with this code number. During the next 30 minutes, derma-toglyphics (palm- and fingerprints) were taken from a sub-set of the families; while this procedure was being carried out, refreshments were offered (day sessions) or a box supper was served (evening sessions). Families were then conducted into the testing auditorium and seated according to a plan designed to keep family groups together but to allow minimal opportunity to see another person's test booklet or to talk. After a brief welcome by a staff member, a tape recording was started that provided test instructions and controlled timing synchronized with 35-mm slides. After the first hour of cognitive tests, a 10-minute recess was given. The test for delayed recall of visual memory was presented just before the recess to prevent possible dis-cussion of the items prior to the re-test. During the second hour testing continued as before. After completion of the cognitive tests, participants were asked to give a saliva sample as they filled out the personal history portion of their questionnaires. As they completed their questionnaires, individuals were invited to turn in all materials and report to a medical technician who with-drew a 20-ml blood sample from each subject. (Blood group, saliva, and dermatoglyphic data are not reported here.) When all members of a family had completed these procedures, the family was given a check for $50, an outline of the research objectives, and forms for referring other qualified and interested families.

ANALYSES

Total sample. Fifteen cognitive scores from the test battery were inter-correlated and subjected to principal component analyses with varimax rotations. Communalities of 1 were used, and the number of factors retained for rotation was set equal to the number of eigenvalues greater than 1 [7]. Factor scores were subsequently computed for each individual.

Ethnic groups. Of those tested, 1971 individuals were Americans of European Ancestry (AEA) and 648 individuals were Americans of Japanese

Ancestry (AJA). Separate factor analyses were conducted on these groups, and within-race factor scores were computed for each individual. No other ethnic group was represented by a sufficient N to be amenable to separate analyses at this time.

Age groups. Separate factor analyses were conducted on the total sample for 12-20, 21-40, and 41-60 age groups.

Results and Discussion

Principal component analyses with varimax rotations confirmed the same four factors reported previously [8] on a sub-sample of this data set. These factors and the common factor loadings of the 15 cognition tests for the total sample are shown in Table 1. Participants with missing data were excluded from factor analyses. The Visual Memory factor loads on only the two (related) tests for recall of items from an array of simple line drawings of familiar items; thus, it is probably the least general of the factors under discussion.

Table 1. Factor Loadings Derived from Total Sample (N = 3074)

| | | Cognitive factor | | |
| | | | | |
Test	Verbal	Spatial Visualization	Perceptual Speed	Visual Memory
1. Vocabulary	76	01	37	01
2. Visual Memory—Immediate	10	09	06	84
3. Things (fluency)	73	19	-09	03
4. Mental Rotations	04	83	-13	08
5. Subtraction & Multiplication	25	06	81	-05
6. Elithorn Mazes	09	60	14	-05
7. Word Beginnings & Endings	65	16	28	07
8. Card Rotations	05	80	11	08
9. Visual Memory—Delayed	07	07	05	85
10. Pedigrees	46	43	41	22
11. Hidden Patterns	28	62	29	08
12. Paper Form Board	39	64	08	07
13. Number Comparisons	08	18	84	15
14. Social Perception—Verbal	65	30	11	15
15. Progressive Matrices—Modified	35	67	10	15
Per cent of Variance	22	18	13	11

Profiles of common factor loadings for the two different ethnic groups (AEA and AJA) are shown in Figure 1. Coefficients of congruence [9] for these groups are as follows: Verbal, 0.99; Spatial Visualization, 0.99; Perceptual Speed and Accuracy, 0.99; and Visual Memory, 0.99. These congruence coefficients are even higher than those reported by DeFries et al. [8] for a sub-sample of these groups, and they furnish further support for the interpretation that the structure of the intellect is essentially identical in these two ethnic groups as represented in Hawaii. Park, Johnson, and Kuse [10] (unpublished) have recently translated the test battery into Korean and administered it to a sample of Korean high school students. The factor structure in this group was highly similar to that reported here and by DeFries et al. [8], although there was an indication that spatial ability was represented by two different factors. Their tentative interpretation of this result is that students who learn to write using the Chinese idiographic or the spatially complex Korean alphabetic system (the lettering runs both from left to right and, within syllables, from top to bottom) develop an aspect of spatial ability which is not usually articulated by those who learn to write in a linearly arranged system.

Comparative factor loading profiles for the three age groups (14-20, 21-40, and 41-60 years) are shown in Figure 2. Coefficients of congruence for the Verbal, Spatial, Perceptual Speed and Accuracy, and Visual Memory factors respectively are: for 14-20 *vs* 21-40, 0.99, 0.99, 0.98, 0.99; for 21-40 *vs* 41-60, 1.00, 1.00, 0.99, 0.99; and for 14-20 *vs* 41-60, 0.99, 0.99, 0.99, 0.99. We conclude that the structure of intellect remains virtually unchanged across the 14-60 age range we have sampled. Though differentiation of abilities must be occurring during childhood, the present data indicate that the process is essentially complete by 14 years of age. The magnitude of these abilities is of course still increasing at this age, as shown below.

Figure 3 shows mean factor scores for males and females separately, for each year of age from 14-20 and in 5-year blocks thereafter. Since the offspring of most families were teenagers, the sample is somewhat deficient for ages 25-35. Table 2 presents the numbers of participants for each age group and for two ethnic groups. (Other ethnic groups were not represented by sufficient numbers of individuals for separate analysis at this time.) Since the factor scores are standardized, with a mean of 0 and variance equal to 1.0, a standard error estimate for any age can be obtained by computing $1/\sqrt{N}$ for that age.

In accordance with most published results, verbal ability shows a rapid increase throughout the teenage years and early 20's and then levels off for most of adult life. The age effect is significant ($F_{13,2950} = 26.09$, p $<$ .001). The dips in the curve at age 18 (males) and age 19 (females) are unexplained, although they may involve lowered motivation in some people within this age group (perhaps as a result of high school graduation) or a sampling bias due to

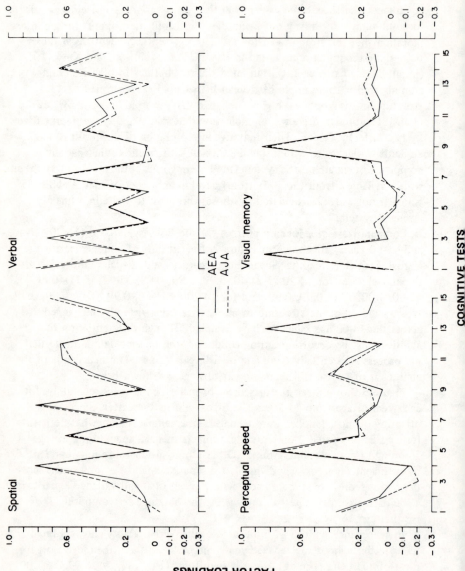

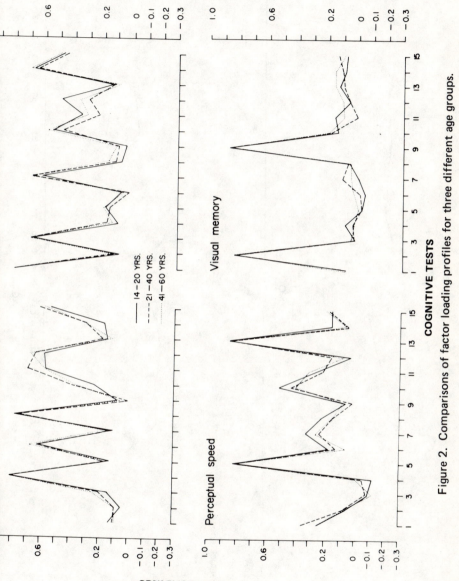

Figure 2. Comparisons of factor loading profiles for three different age groups.

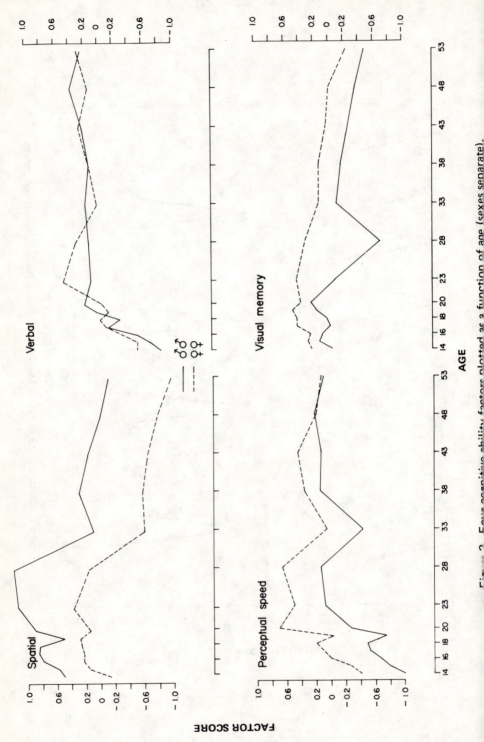

Figure 2. Four cognitive ability factors plotted as a function of age (sexes separate).

Table 2. Number of Subjects with Complete Test Data
For the Age and Ethnic Groups Shown

								Age group						
	14	15	16	17	18	19	20	21-25	26-30	31-35	36-40	41-45	46-50	51-55
Total males	72	135	127	120	49	15	30	32	7	24	234	283	230	99
Total females	72	162	128	99	64	25	17	46	12	84	278	295	176	63
Total AEA	95	198	162	131	66	19	22	39	10	97	415	356	233	82
Total AJA	22	43	43	32	25	10	11	22	5	1	45	140	124	50

non-inclusion in our sample of many who had entered colleges away from home. No overall sex differences were observed; however, there may be a tendency for females to develop verbal ability somewhat earlier (sex $\times$ age interaction: $F_{13,2950} = 1.69$, p $< .10$).

As shown in Figure 3, there was a large and consistent sex difference in spatial ability ($F_{1,2950} = 184.0$, p $< .001$) as well as a reliable age trend ($F_{13,2950} = 45.4$, p $< .001$). The sex difference was somewhat smaller in the younger groups (age $\times$ sex interaction: $F_{13,2950} = 1.89$, p $< .05$). Again, there were deviations in the function at ages 18 and 19 and, perhaps, at age 33 (30-35). The latter deviation may be due to unreliability due to small sample size. Alternatively, it may be a function of real differences, as parents in this age range who were able to bring in a 14-year-old offspring must have been married at an unusually early age and may differ from others in education and/or ability. Despite the large sex differences shown, daughters (females aged 14-28) had spatial ability scores very similar to those of their fathers (males aged 33-60), although their scores were much lower than those of their brothers (males aged 14-28). Many women (33-60) seemed to find tests of spatial ability quite difficult and rather stressful, as was evident from remarks during testing and the recess. Whether these empirical observations are due to sex chromosome differences, hormonal differences, differences in sex role training, or other experiential differences (or a combination of reasons), they seem to be quite consistent and real.

There are both age and sex differences on the remaining two factors, with young adults and females achieving higher scores. For the Perceptual Speed and Accuracy factor, despite deviations at 18, 19 and 33 years noted also for the Spatial factor, there is a significant age effect ($F_{13,2950} = 28.7$, p $< .001$). This effect is due mainly to the increase in this ability during the teenage years, as only a modest decrement is seen at older ages. The sex difference is reliable ($F_{1,2950} = 77.3$, p $< .001$), although it diminishes with age and vanishes at about age 45 (sex $\times$ age interaction: $F_{13,2950} = 4.0$, p $< .001$). The Visual

Memory factor shows a clear sex difference in favor of females ($F_{1,2950} = 36.0$, $p < .001$) and a significant ($F_{13,2950} = 7.2$, $p < .001$) age trend (sex $\times$ age interaction: $F_{13,2950} = 0.68$, N.S.).

Although included in the factors discussed above, results for four of the specific tests employed are presented in Figure 4 for those who prefer to examine functions involving particular test scores rather than somewhat hypothetical factors. The four tests are: PMA Vocabulary, a measure of crystallized intelligence; Raven's Progressive Matrices, a measure of fluid intelligence; Sheppard-Metzler-Vandenberg Mental Rotations, a fairly new and fairly difficult measure of spatial ability; and Visual Memory—Delayed, a measure of memory or retention. The age trend for PMA Vocabulary is very similar to that shown for the Verbal factor, with somewhat more indication of higher scores for females. Essentially no drop is seen within the age range sampled, which is in accordance with previous findings [11]. The age trend for Progressive Matrices scores is interesting in that decline with age is more evident than for any other test or any factor except Spatial. This is consistent with previous findings [11] and lends support to the hypothesis that fluid intelligence declines with age. Progressive Matrices was administered as a power test, with a comfortably long time limit, so the decrement is probably not due to the relative inability or unwillingness of older people to respond to speed tests [12, 13]. A sex difference is also evident, with males achieving higher scores. The results for Mental Rotations are similar to those for the Spatial factor, although sex differences are even more evident. Results for the Visual Memory—Delayed test are quite similar to those for the Visual Memory factor. The significance values for specific tests are shown in Table 3.

One of the most consistent features of the obtained age curves is the very rapid development of tested abilities during the early teenage years. We had chosen age 14 as the lower criterion for taking these adult-form tests, with the expectation that those 14 or older would have adult or nearly adult levels of ability on these tests. It is now apparent that age adjustments will be required before proceeding with other planned analyses.

Also noteworthy are the relatively high mean factor scores obtained at about age 20. Perhaps these high scores represent full development of ability, along with school-developed expertise in test taking, high motivation and excellent health. A gradual decline after the peak at about age 20 can be discerned for several of the factors and tests. A decline as early as the late 20's and early 30's would be somewhat surprising, but by no means impossible. The data make a strong case that this may be so for spatial ability; the decline after a peak in the late teens is consistent in both sexes and both ethnic groups.

Because of the congruity of factor structures in our two major ethnic groups, within-race factor scores were computed for each individual for presentation as a function of age. This was done in an attempt to bring into sharper focus changes in test or factor scores which were ostensibly age re-

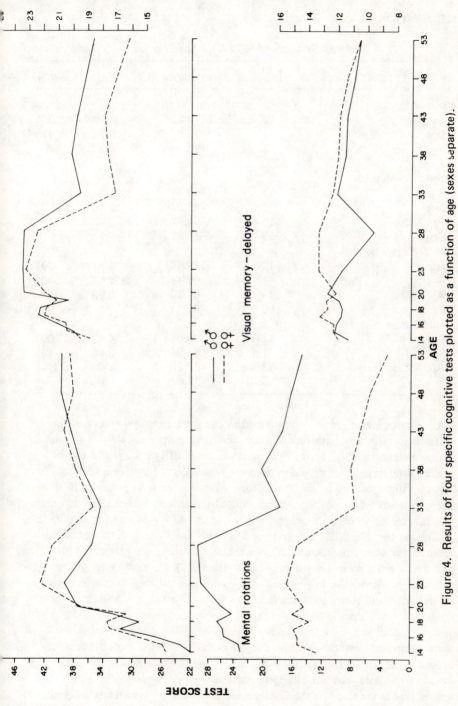

Figure 4. Results of four specific cognitive tests plotted as a function of age (sexes separate).

125

Table 3. Results of ANOVA for Specific Tests

	df	Mean Square	F	p ⩽
Vocabulary				
Age	13	7377.2	80.64	.001
Sex	1	635.5	6.95	.01
Age X Sex	13	125.7	1.37	NS
Error	2950	91.5		
Progressive Matrices				
Age	13	452.81	21.27	.001
Sex	1	288.59	13.55	.001
Age X Sex	13	51.72	2.43	.01
Error	2950	21.28		
Mental Rotations				
Age	13	3589.6	36.87	.001
Sex	1	32566.4	334.54	.001
Age X Sex	13	67.10	0.69	NS
Error	2950	97.34		
Visual Memory—Delayed				
Age	13	185.67	14.42	.001
Sex	1	44.94	3.49	.10
Age X Sex	13	12.95	1.00	NS
Error	2950	12.87		

lated. Use of factor scores computed from the total sample would result in differences reflecting both race and age. Since we cannot equate the samples for proficiency in English or in taking tests, these differences would not be readily interpretable. It should perhaps be noted that neither race had consistently higher scores on all four factors. When figures were prepared to show age trends within races, there was an evident interaction between age and race, but sample N's were too small (especially for the AJA group and in the 20-35 age range) to yield stable estimates or a smooth function. Accordingly, we reduced the age comparison to only two points, a mean for offspring (14-20 years old) and a mean for parents (36-60 years old), for each factor. These relationships are shown in Figure 5. The age X race interaction now emerges very clearly, and it is significant for every factor (Verbal: t = 5.56, p < .001; Spatial: t = 5.97, p < .001; Speed: t = 1.96, p < .05; Memory: t = 2.11, p < .05; all df = 2,366). It should be clearly understood that factor scores were computed separately within race, so each line plotted must balance around a mean of 0 (weighted by N); the relevant comparison is the angle between the lines, not, for example, point to point comparison by ethnic group. Nor is the slope of the lines a good indication of age trends, since the initial point plotted is the mean factor score for ages 14-20 and many of the

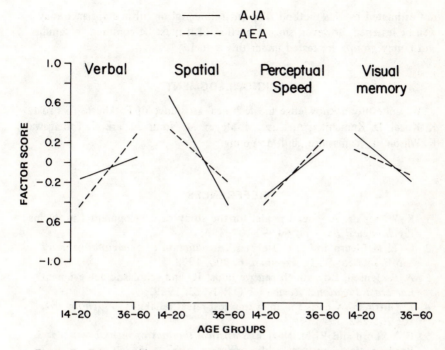

Figure 5. Ethnicity X age interactions for four cognitive ability factors.

younger offspring had not yet achieved their full potential. Nevertheless, this seems a useful way of highlighting the age X race interaction for these two ethnic groups. The significant interaction may represent a different rate of development and/or decline of abilities in the two groups, different educational opportunities, or some combination of these effects. More data will be needed to address these questions usefully.

Botwinick [14] has summarized many of the criticisms which have been made of both cross-sectional and longitudinal research designs for age comparisons. Although neither is free from fault, both are still being used. Schaie [1] has presented a general model for the study of developmental problems. This model allows estimation of age trends, corrected for cultural and genetic changes which may be occurring during the time sampled; however, it is somewhat expensive in time and money. An extension of the cross-sectional model to include a genetic control, such as that used in our study, may provide a useful research design. It would seem to control for any possible genetic changes, since all the genes in the offspring group are replicate samples derived from the parental group represented on the same age curve. Cultural changes, especially those usually termed "cohort differences," must in general be assumed to be possible sources of variance not estimated by this method. The environmental or cultural variance may well be lessened, however, since a portion of it must be common to families, and family *groups* are tested under this model.

ACKNOWLEDGMENT

We gratefully acknowledge the technical assistance of F. Ahern, C. Frost, K. Kocel, D. Kunichika, A. Kuse, M. Meyer, M. Nomi, J. Park, J. Tamagawa, K. Wilson, T. Yamashita, and M. Young.

REFERENCES

1. K. W. Schaie, A general model for the study of developmental problems. *Psychological Bulletin,* 64: 92-107, 1965.
2. G. E. McClearn and J. C. DeFries, *Introduction to behavioral genetics.* San Francisco: W. H. Freeman, p. 206, 1973.
3. A. R. Jensen, How much can we boost IQ and scholastic achievement? *Harvard Educational Review,* 39(1): 1-123, 1969.
4. L. Guttman, A basis for analyzing test-retest reliability. *Psychometrika,* 10: 255-282, 1945.
5. F. M. Lord and R. M. Novick, *Statistical theories of mental test scores.* Reading, Massachusetts: Addison-Wesley, p. 87, 1968.
6. S. G. Vandenberg and W. Meredith, The selection of a test battery for a study of genetic and environmental components in cognition; a partial replication of the fluid-crystallized distinction among abilities. Submitted.
7. H. F. Kaiser, The application of electronic computers to factor analysis. *Educational and Psychological Measurement,* 20: 141-151, 1960.
8. J. C. DeFries, S. G. Vandenberg, G. E. McClearn, A. R. Kuse, J. R. Wilson, G. C. Ashton and R. C. Johnson. Near identity of cognitive structure in two ethnic groups. *Science,* 183: 338-339, 1974.
9. L. R. Tucker, *Personnel Research Section Report No. 984.* Washington, D.C.: Department of the Army, 1951.
10. J. Y. Park, R. C. Johnson and A. R. Kuse, Cognition structures in two different cultures. Unpublished.
11. R. B. Cattell, The structure of intelligence in relation to the nature-nurture controversy. In R. Cancro, Ed., *Intelligence: Genetic and environmental influences.* New York: Grune and Stratton, p. 12, 1971.
12. K. Barton, Recent data on the culture fair scales. In *Technical Supplement for the Culture Fair Intelligence Tests Scales 2 and 3.* Champaign, Illinois: Institute for Personality and Ability Testing, 1973.
13. J. E. Birren, K. F. Riegel and D. F. Morrison, Analysis of the WAIS subtests in relation to age and education. *Journal of Gerontology,* 16: 363-369, 1961.
14. J. Botwinick, Geropsychology. *Annual Review of Psychology,* 21: 239-272, 1970.

chapter 10

RETIREMENT
TO THE PORCH
IN RURAL APPALACHIA[1]

John Lozier
Ronald Althouse

A front porch is useless for most Americans. New houses are built with a vestigial stoop in front, and outdoor leisure life focuses on the backyard or patio. The wide front porches of older houses often stand empty, if they have not been enclosed to provide more "useful" interior space.

In Laurel Creek, West Virginia, front porches are still in use, although their significance may be declining [1]. People of any age may use the front porch, but its special importance for old people is shown in the photographic cliche of the old man sitting in a rocking chair. Although it is a stereotype, this image reflects a real culture process, which we call "retirement to the porch." This paper

[1] This research was supported by grants from West Virginia University Faculty Senate and from the Office of Research and Development, Appalachian Center, WVU. An earlier version of this paper was presented at the Central States Anthropological Society Meetings, Chicago, March 27-29, 1974.

129

deals mainly with males who make use of the porch much more extensively than do females.

Our aim here is to describe the process of retirement to the porch in Laurel Creek, showing how it follows from a long-time participation in a particular kind of social system. We do not think of this process merely as a peculiar cultural characteristic of Appalachia; it can be observed in many rural, small-town, and even urban neighborhoods where front porches continue to be used. Beyond a description of the process, we want to give some illustrations of how an old person may use the front porch to maintain a public presence in his community, to continue to press his social claims, to execute his remaining social obligations, and to provide the community with an opportunity to make arrangements for his eventual demise.

Laurel Creek is a rural community of about 200 households, situated near the Kentucky border in Southern West Virginia. The original settlers who came just after the revolutionary war lived by agriculture, but in the present century timbering and then mining became the principal economic activities. This is an economically distressed area, and emigration in early adulthood has left the population disproportionately distributed in young and old age categories.

Throughout his lifetime, one major social obligation of a male is to secure and to maintain steady employment. Economic conditions have made this exceedingly difficult for most people, and a history of periodic unemployment is characteristic of almost all mature and old men.[2] Given the experience of periodic unemployment, the best that a man can do is to publicly display his energy, skill, and readiness to work, which provide him with good standing and access to work when it becomes available.

A mature man, when not at work on a job, may spend his time in job-seeking activity away from the house, or he may work about his house and yard, or he may engage in non-productive leisure activities. As long as he is steadily employed, his time at home may include considerable non-productive leisure, but if he is unemployed, it may be very important for him to demonstrate his industry through activities such as gardening, house repair and improvement, tending the yard, and so forth. For this reason, a mature male does not normally spend much time sitting in apparent idleness on the front porch. He may use the porch as a place to entertain visitors, for family interaction, or for reading, but any extensive display of solitary sitting on the porch implies that he is retiring from active life, that he no longer seeks or requires further steady employment. Thus a man who appears to be retiring may primarily experience social pressure to behave more appropriately.

[2] Intensive interviews based on a sample of every other household on Laurel Creek (n = 81) indicated that 49% of the household heads not yet of retirement age had enjoyed steady employment during the preceding five-year period, while the remaining families encountered periodic unemployment or dropped from the labor force.

The Process of Retirement to the Porch

Retirement to the porch begins to become apparent when a man is freed of the obligation to work steadily away from home. The obligation to work is conventionally assumed to end at age 65, when a man may receive social security.[3] Given the expectation of periodic unemployment, and the difficulty which men in their late 50's and early 60's have in finding work, most find themselves forced into retirement and an intermittent or occasional work pattern well before age 65.

When an aging man is assumed to be no longer competing for steady work, he may begin to spend more time on the front porch. Ideally, this early-retirement period is a time when the man has the freedom to pick and choose his work activities. Typically he would spend a considerable amount of his time at home engaged in work about the house and yard, but he is free to spend time on the porch without damaging consequences, since it is assumed that he will no longer be considered for steady work. From the front porch, he can observe the flow of activity on the road, and he can exchange information with those who stop. He may move freely from the porch to the more public places at the main forks of Laurel or in the nearby town, perhaps riding in with someone who has come by. This kind of social interaction provides him with opportunities to arrange occasional work, or unpaid assistance in some project that provides social interaction and helps to maintain his social standing. As long as he is active and able, it is important that he continue to be available to help others and to provide for himself, associating with others in a way that is established from patterns of reciprocity in earlier years.

Full retirement to the porch comes when a man's participation in activities beyond the house and yard is no longer considered necessary, perhaps because health is failing, or perhaps because others are able to relieve him of the obligations on him. This is a time when a man begins to accept the idea of being dependent on others, when he ceases to actively accumulate further social credit and, instead, draws on the credit already achieved. Instead of using the porch as a spring board to occasional involvement in the activities of others, he increasingly remains on the porch, and others come to him. He still may spend some time working in the yard, but this is likely to be purely maintenance activity, or casual "puttering about." His relative immobility becomes socially acknowledged, and he becomes privileged to request service from others who may pass by—the delivery of groceries or tobacco, or a few moments of conversation. Whereas in the early porch retirement, a passer-by might acknowledge the old man with a

[3] Workingmen in settlements such as Laurel Creek may be physically disabled fairly early in their maturity or otherwise experience retirement from work in local industries which is quite abrupt. For some data pertaining to age of disabling injury and retirement, see D. S. Hall, R. Althouse, and E. Bosanac, "Health-Related Characteristics of Persons Living in Areas Served by the Wharton and Rainelle Medical Centers: A Preliminary Report," West Virginia Regional Medical Program, Morgantown, West Virginia, 1973.

nod or a brief greeting, as he becomes more immobilized the obligation becomes stronger for the passer-by to stop and chat, to offer service, or to come up on the porch to sit a while. The old man may ask children to run errands for him, and their response may be reported favorably or unfavorably to their parents or others in the community.

As strength continues to fail, the old man may find it increasingly difficult to do even the minimal work about the house and yard. Porched now for real, the maintenance of the yard becomes an obligation of others, often kin but sometimes other neighbors. Though others in the community continue to be under obligation to stop and greet him, it is assumed that he may be tired by conversation, and his companionship comes from a more restricted set of kin who come visiting or from his wife. In this condition, he may remain for an indefinite time, his needs increasingly supplied by a society of close kin and his requests and desires communicated by them on his behalf.

If he has reached this point without any dramatic incidents, it now becomes more and more likely that he will experience periodic health crises which prevent him from emerging from the house to the porch. If he does not appear on the porch, this is immediately noticed and communicated, and before long the community learns of his condition and prognosis from someone close to him.

When he reappears on the porch after periodic crises, he is "recuperating," and the expectation is that other crises will come before long. Consequently, there is an increased urgency about providing him with appropriate social inter-action while he is on the porch. After each reappearance on the porch, he en-joys a brief flurry of special attention as people come to greet him; and although there is perhaps no clear sign regarding the length of time he may have remaining, the assumption that he will not regain full strength provides a justification for permitting him whatever indulgence he may desire—a drink, a smoke, a degree of excitement that may give him pleasure even though it may be medically damaging.

At some point, the old man never recovers sufficiently to resume a routine of appearance on the porch. The community networks provide a running assess-ment of his condition, and the prognosis becomes negative. He is now socially defined as being in a terminal state. Now, with the expectation that he will die before long, it is likely that an opportunity will be sought, on a warm day when he is feeling better, and he will be brought out again to the porch. Now, instead of being in "recuperation," he is described as "sick on the porch." Whereas the reappearance for "recuperation" is not a matter for urgent communication, notice of appearance on the porch in a terminal condition is rapidly broadcast, and for a couple of hours, perhaps, he will be receiving his final public attention. Withdrawn again to the house, he will be cared for by the more restricted society of kin and close friends until his death.

Social Conditions and Support: How Porch-Users Fare

Although retirement to the porch provides a comforting ideal for the elder years, complete success is difficult to achieve in practice. For about 25 per cent of the old people in Laurel Creek, who have spent their lifetimes outside the community and returned only in old age, social networks are relatively weak, and a presence on the porch does not call for a community response as it would for one who had been a lifelong resident. These people, whom we have called "cash-ins," tend not to display porch behavior; indeed, they frequently live in mobile homes or other dwellings which do not even have porches.

For those who have spent the bulk of their careers within the community, retirement to the porch is frequently not possible for other reasons. Implicit in the concept of retirement to the porch is the idea that the individual has managed to accumulate a degree of social standing that justifies his claims for support from the community at large. Not all elders have developed this kind of social standing. Some are simply "no-counts," people who have never been regarded as valued members of the community, and for whom the absence of legitimate claims in old age is but a continuation of such a situation in earlier life. Others have developed their personal careers more narrowly within a society of kinsmen, and for them, the services and resources they require in old age are not heavily involved with the community at large; thus appearances on the porch, if they occur, do not have the social meaning outlined earlier.

Still another factor that may prevent a retirement to the porch is unusual success for an individual. In one notable case, a very successful man, who had served as teacher, school principal, preacher, storekeeper, and political intermediary, found when he sold his store and attempted to retire that the requests for his services were so extensive that he came back out of retirement; he repurchased his store and continued to work actively until very near his death, concealing the fact that he had terminal cancer.

Retirement to the porch is therefore most typical of persons who have achieved a solid degree of social standing, but whose capacity to continue in active exchange with others begins to fail in old age.

An illustration of a fully effective retirement to the porch may be seen in the case of Fred Chaplin. Fred and his wife Edna lived some distance up the left fork of Laurel Creek; situated as they were, the normal traffic on the road included only other local residents, but Fred was relatively fit, and he could easily arrange for a ride to the main forks with passers-by, who rarely failed to pass the time of day with him when he was on the porch. Fred always had a reason to go to town—he would have a bill to pay or a purchase to make—and these "excuses" could provide him with a justification for making a request whenever an opportunity was presented. The request was never an imposition on the passer-by, because after all he was going there anyway.

Fred had about five acres of excellent bottom land just across the road from his porch. In earlier life, he worked all or most of it, but now as he retired more fully to the porch, he would negotiate for others to use it. One year he rented it, but he didn't like having the transaction purely financial; he felt, perhaps correctly, that it provided a better return when it was used in a more generalized social exchange. In the Spring, he would hitch up his mule and plow a few furrows along one edge, then leave the plow standing there in plain sight from the porch. The evidence of the beginning of work simply could not fail to provoke comment in any conversation he might have from the porch, and before long he would have negotiated with one or more others to prepare gardens on the land.

Fred and Edna continued to display an interest in maintaining and improving their home. One day a new bathtub and commode were delivered, and they were placed in a conspicuous spot right up front on the porch. They remained there for about three weeks, during which time talk focused on his plans, and then three men from up the hollow came in and helped him to install them in the house.

Those who do not live in traditional communities, even social scientists, often make the casual assumption that everyone in such communities knows everyone else's business. While this may serve as a general statement, in reality some individuals know far more than others within such a system. Many of the younger people at the head of Laurel knew little of the circumstances of their neighbors, for their daily routines did not bring them together. But everyone talked to Fred and Edna Chaplin, and as a consequence, these two knew a great deal about them all. Fred might observe to a passer-by that so-and-so had returned for a visit, but where was his wife? Well, she was working, and so-and-so had time off, so he came home for a visit. Or, they had quarreled and separated. Fred and Edna could collect such information, sift it and check it for consistency, and then re-introduce it into the stream of communications, always selectively and at their own discretion. From the porch, Fred's questions had an element of demand in them, as it would be improper not to reply to one whose mobility and access to information was presumed to be restricted. On the other hand, Fred was under no particular pressure to provide information in response to the questions of others. Any fieldworker will immediately recognize how valuable the confidence of such a person would be.

Wallace Meadows had an active and creditable career, but he never achieved a command of the porch in his old age. His own two sons migrated, and rejected his assistance to bring them home and fix them in jobs, because his demands on them were overly taxing. As a daughter-in-law said of a period when she and her husband lived across the road from Wallace, "there was no front door on our house," claiming the presumed privilege of the patriarch to demand service on his own terms and his own schedule, Wallace placed a burden on his family that was generally considered to be excessive.

Like numerous other old people whose children are not residing in Laurel Creek, Wallace attempted to use the porch as a place from which to present his claims and to participate in the community beyond his direct kin. Such a strategy is by no means doomed to failure. However, Wallace expected too much of others, and his claims seemed more to be demands than requests. If he would ask for a ride in to the main forks, he might want to stop repeatedly, or to take the driver out of his way, making the act of service relatively costly; and in exchange he could give little. With such a pattern of behavior emerging, passers-by increasingly gave evasive indications of their plans, and discouraged him from coming along.

From the porch, old men often make small requests of boys who may pass by, perhaps bicycling to the main forks, asking for tobacco or an item of grocery. No strong sanction forces the child to respond, but the boy who performs creditably is likely to be praised, to his parents and to others in the community. If the relationship between the old man and the child's father is sufficiently close, word of misbehavior by the child is likely to result in scolding or punishment by his parents. Wallace appeared to assume that he could legitimately demand service of this kind from children in the neighborhood, and when performance was not up to Wallace's expectations, Wallace was quick to inform the child's parents, but due to his growing reputation for oppressive demands, the parents would not provide the necessary control on their children. More and more, children as well as adults avoided making themselves available to him.

The public view appears to have been that since Wallace was still mobile, and since by his demanding style he implied that he could still control social sanctions on his own behalf, he could not expect the community to support him in retirement to the porch. He was thus forced back off the porch and into active participation. In the future, failing health and decreased mobility might provide him with a justification for retiring to the porch, but to the extent that he continues to behave as a "contentious old son of a bitch," his ultimate retirement to the porch is likely to be socially supported at a much lower level than he would want. Stated otherwise, he is "using up" his social credit, and will find himself in a relatively insecure position later on.

For people who have not resided within the community throughout their work life, the opportunity to accumulate social credit is limited. Sanford Tanner spent his career outside Laurel Creek and returned in retirement. He owned property there and was recognized as a community member, but his assets were mainly in the form of cash claims—pension and savings. He did spend time on the porch prior to his death, but this was not sufficient to provide him with the basis for making claims for support. Rather, he was forced to negotiate for the services he needed, exchanging cash or valuable property.

Tanner was already quite sick when he returned, and he needed regular care. This was provided by a neighbor woman, Audrey Dooley. She did not take cash; rather, she presented her behavior as a Christian service. However, Audrey's three daughters and their husbands, all living nearby, provided a good deal of help to Tanner, and these younger people did receive payment, sometimes cash and sometimes gifts. One son-in-law, for example, got Tanner's car, with the assumption that this provided the old man with transportation when he needed it.

In the spring of the year before he died, Tanner appeared on the porch quite regularly, but that summer he became sick, and his failure to reappear signalled that he was indeed terminal. The community then became actively concerned to work out the proper arrangements for his death and for the inheritance of his property. As for his personal needs, little public interest was evident, although there was some concern about whether Audrey Dooley and her family were the proper people to care for him in his terminal condition. This concern was ultimately based in the public interest in a proper disposal of the property, which was apparently being "claimed" by the Dooley family. When he died, it was indeed learned that he had willed his house and land to Audrey Dooley. Although there was some disgruntled response, this disposition of the property was rapidly provided with the mantle of respectability; religious leaders in the community provided support for the view that Audrey's service had been substantial and proper and that she was entitled to receive the inheritance.

Because he had not accumulated social claims within the community, Tanner's appearance on the porch had little social significance beyond the fact that he continued to survive; but this was indeed an important message, because it notified the community of his continuing needs. His disappearance from the porch, signalling terminal condition, notified the community of the impending matter of disposing of his estate.

The Absence of Social Support: When Porches "Don't Work"

As an illustration of a course toward death that does not involve retirement to the porch, we may briefly note the case of Elwood Howard. Howard had purchased property in Laurel Creek in his early adulthood and raised four children who emigrated, although they remained in the region. After the death of his wife, Howard became sick, and he employed a woman from a nearby small town to care for him. As he became sicker, the two married, and the wife continued to care for him, now without the implication of direct cash payment. At Howard's death, his second wife was designated as heir by his will. The will was contested unsuccessfully by Howard's own children.

Elwood Howard in his later years was virtually invisible in the community, even though he lived within a hundred yards of the main forks. His house did not even have a porch, but if it had, his appearance on it would have signalled no social claims. His children had all gone, and his own roots were not deep in the community. As far as the community was concerned, his death would not affect the community, as they fully anticipated that the property would be inherited by outsiders and that it would very likely be up for sale. This was indeed the case; the wife sold out and left within six months of his death.

Conclusion

The theoretical approach we are attempting to develop has been called "societal," concerned with "how . . . society organizes and behaves with reference to its older people" [2]. Our analysis is based upon the assumption that 1) old people have legitimate claims, 2) others are obligated in general and specific ways to old people, and 3) society enforces the claims of old people by sanctioning the behavior of juniors.

In this paper, we attempt to show how the claims of an old person may be kept in evidence through the semi-public appearance on the front porch. It is important to emphasize, however, that use of the porch creates no claims, but rather facilitates the assertion of claims which are already developed in advance.

Porch behavior need not be absent in urban settings, and where porches are not present or used, there may be other ways that an aging person may keep his claims in evidence before a relevant public. Generally, however, it is very much more difficult for an individual to develop and to maintain social credit in a social environment where the personnel are transient; if neighbors change, then no record remains of the service of those who are left in isolation.

The problem is poignantly illustrated by the experience of a relative of one of the authors. This aging woman, isolated from kin in an urban neighborhood, presents herself as a "Christian woman," displaying great concern for the needs of older people who are more frail than she. Often she calls on younger people in the neighborhood to provide services for these needy old people. She is attempting to be a kind of patroness, developing a pattern of neighborhood support for old people. As she herself grows older and requires more support from neighbors, she would like to be able to rely on the community to recognize her past service and to return her due reward with dignity, but she seems plainly fearful that this may not happen.

The problem of providing for old people in modern society is not simply a question of providing services. What is required for successful old age is the continuing existence of community or neighborhood systems which can recognize and store credit for the performance of an individual over a whole lifetime and which can enforce the obligation of juniors to provide reciprocity. Without such a system, the help that is provided to an elder robs him of his dignity, for there is no recognition that this is his due, and not a form of charity.

REFERENCES

1. Lozier, John and Althouse, Ronald. "Social Enforcement of Behavior Toward Elders in an Appalachian Mountain Settlement," *The Gerontologist*, 14:1, 69-80, 1974.
2. Tibbitts, C. "Origin, Scope and Fields of Social Gerontology." In C. Tibbitts, *Handbook on Social Gerontology*. Chicago: University of Chicago Press, 1960.

chapter 11

THE BLACKLANDS
OF GERONTOLOGY[1]

Jacquelyne Johnson Jackson, Ph.D.[2]

Previous visits to *The Blacklands of Gerontology* (Jackson, 1967; 1971*a*) have focused largely upon a presentation and critique of selected literature pertinent to aging and aged blacks, emphasizing especially the paucity *and* inconclusive findings of much of the available data, emergent issues arising therefrom (such as those of relationships between and among race, aging, religion, family and kinship, and health, as well as methodological ones principally concerned with inadequate conceptualizations and collection and interpretation of the data), the usually low socioeconomic statuses of black aged, and critical research and social policy needs. This third visit falls within the same genre, since it provides an additional bibliographic collection and commentary. It also permits a limited assessment of trends in research and factors affecting research on black aged, 1950-1971.

THE STATE OF THE LITERATURE

In general, *The Blacklands of Gerontology* are more fertile than they were two decades ago as there has been a continuing and slowly proliferating availability of more heterogeneous literature on black aged. More black subjects are being included in study populations containing white subjects, with a tendency (still conspicuously absent in some cases) of increasing sampling sizes to permit more sophisticated data analyses by race, as well as the very important trend of restricting samples to black subjects alone. This allows isolation of similarities and differences among processes of black aging, clearly recognizing (as many still do not) that blacks are highly variable.

A greater emphasis and concern is being given to minority aged (including blacks) by The Gerontological Society, as exemplified by its sponsorship of roundtable discussions on minorities at recent annual meetings and the special series of articles on elderly minorities in *The Gerontologist*, 11:26-98, 1971. The National Council on Aging has also pursued field work among minority elderly funded largely by the office of Economic Opportunity, and focused on them at its Annual Conference, March, 1971. The Institute of Gerontology at The University of Michigan-Wayne State University shows increased inclusion of minority group students in training programs and recently held a Symposium

[1] This paper was partially supported by the U. S. Public Health Service, Grant #MH1655402, and by the Center for the Study of Aging and Human Development, Duke University Medical Center, Durham, North Carolina, Grant 5 TO1 HD00164 of the National Institute of Child Health and Human Development.
[2] Assistant professor of medical sociology, Department of Psychiatry, Duke University Medical Center, Durham, North Carolina, 27706. Special acknowledgement is made of the bibliographic and other assistance rendered especially by Shirley Bagley (NICHD); Henry Norwood and Peter Hobbes (research assistants); the National Center for Health Statistics, under the directions of Dr. Theodore Woolsey; Daniel I. Rubenstein (Brandeis University); Robert Kastenbaum (Wayne State University); and Viola E. Jackson (my daughter who entertained herself begrudgingly so that I could complete this task).

on "Triple Jeopardy: The Plight of Age Minorities in America," April, 1971. The Gerontological Center at the University of Southern California has been making training contributions, sought involvement in various community programs, and developed a Workshop on Ethnicity, Mental Health, and Aging. The significant contributions of the U. S. Senate Special Committee on Aging under the direction of William Oriol include its temporary contract with Dr. Inabel Lindsay to provide a systematic review of available knowledge on black aged.

A small but growing band of black gerontologists and other blacks interested in the aged has emerged[3]. There has been continuing interest and activities underfoot by the National Urban League to conduct research on and promote concern for the black aged. There is a strong possibility that the Administration on Aging, U. S. Department of Health, Education, and Welfare, will fund, for the first time, a gerontological training program at a black institution (probably at Fisk University where adequate personnel are already available and/or Tennessee State University, both in Nashville) which should contribute significantly towards a reduction of the shortage of trained black researchers and service-providers.

A *Research Conference on Minority Group Aged in the South* is planned, to be funded by the National Institute of Child Health and Development, to permit a systematic assessment of the current status of research on the black aged, tentatively scheduled for early October, Nashville, Tennessee. Perhaps the most important development is the formation of the *National Caucus on the Black Aged* in November, 1970, under the leadership of Hobart C. Jackson (Chief Administrator, the Stephen Smith Geriatric Center, Philadelphia) and Robert J. Kastenbaum (Director, Center for the Study of Death, Dying and Lethal Behavior, Wayne State University).

It is significant that those responsible for planning the forthcoming 1971 White House Conference on Aging failed to provide for policy formulations focusing specifically upon the acute problems and needs of minority group aged, especially those who are in "quadruple jeopardy" by being black and female and old and poor. This glaring omission particularly as it relates to critical needs in the areas of housing, income, health, and retirement roles and activities, should be corrected. A step in this direction may well be a possible *National Conference on Black Aged*, tentatively scheduled for Washington, D.C., November, 1971. The organization of an effective and permanent "Committee of One Hundred Elderly Black Statesmen," composed largely of those sixty-five or more years of age who have had active professional and civic careers, could do much to spark the needed attention upon the deplorable plight of many black elderly. It would certainly provide a "Black House" of cogent policies for legislative and other remedies.

Despite the fertility of *The Blacklands of Gerontology*, certain critical research,

---

[3] I am often among those asked to identify black gerontologists and/or those behavorial scientists interested in aging. A partial listing would include Dr. Stanley H. Smith (Fisk University); Dr. James E. Blackwell (University of Massachusetts at Boston); Dr. Maurice Jackson (University of Southern California); Dr. Robert Staples (University of California, Irvine); Miss Gloria Walker and Mrs. Marguerite Howie (South Carolina State College); Dr. Wilbur Watson (Rutgers University and the Stephen Smith Geriatric Center, Philadelphia); Dr. Hubert Ross (Atlanta University); Dr. Jesse Gloster (Texas Southern University); Dr. Barbara Solomon (University of Southern California); Dr. James E. Conyers (Indiana State University, Terre Haute); Dr. Ralph H. Hines (Meharry Medical College); Dr. Adelbert H. Jenkins (New York University); Dr. Charles U. Smith (Florida A. and M. University); Dr. Floyd Wylie (Wayne State University); Dr. Robert Hill (National Urban League, Washington, D.C.); Dr. Inabel Lindsay (Washington, D.C.), Mr. Abraham Davis, Jr. (HEW, Washington, D.C.); Dr. Percil Stanford; and Mrs. Mercerdee Thompson (St. Louis).

training, and service needs, remain extant. These have been identified, particularly by Bourg (1971), Havighurst (1971), H. Jackson (1971), J. Jackson (1967; 1970; 1971a; 1971b; 1971c), Jenkins (1971), Kalish (1971), Kastenbaum (1971), and Kent (1971a, 1971b; 1971c), as well as the issue of the implications of recent black militancy on the psychological well-being of aged blacks dividing Elam (1970) and Solomon (1970). These attest to the need for carefully executed, intensive, interdisciplinary studies employing national, random samples of aging and aged blacks. Also needed are an enlarged cadre of gerontologists (especially black) focusing upon black aged, substantial training and research funds for this research, crucial improvements in the services available to black aged, and their satisfactory utilization of such services. Almost all of the behavioral scientists cited recognize the critical and varying impacts of racial discrimination upon aging.

This literature review, with some notable exceptions, is restricted to what has become available within the last several years, as well as certain projections about what is likely to be available within the next year. The search is not exhaustive, and additional information on existing and projected literature and demonstration and service projects would be particularly welcomed. The four areas to be investigated in this review are aging and: (a) health, life expectancy, and race; (b) psychology and race; (c) social patterns, policies, and resources; and (d) additional related information.

HEALTH, LIFE EXPECTANCY, AND RACE

The bulk of the literature under consideration relates directly or indirectly to: (1) physical and mental health; (2) factors affecting the delivery and utilization of health-care services; (3) racial differentials in body age, life expectancy, and mortality; and (4) aged sexual behavior.

Physical and mental health. All available data tend to suggest that black males seventy-five or more years of age tend to be in better health than their female or white counterparts. This fact may be attributed to the much earlier deaths of black males who were physiologically, psychologically, and socioculturally less advantaged. Aging blacks are afflicted by various health disabilities associated with increasing age. However there is still need for a careful study of their physical and mental health in later years.

The National Center for Health Statistics has published some limited, but useful data on health patterns of blacks. Included in the most recent National Health Surveys, beginning around 1959, are statistics from medical examinations performed upon a probability sample of noninstitutionalized persons, eighteen to seventy-nine years of age, and later with the Health Interview Surveys. Plans are underfoot to examine the available data systematically. Table 1 provides some selected data on health characteristics of black and white males and females in varying age groupings. These data from the National Health Examination Survey tend to support the expected racial variations in health conditions. They also reveal certain interesting lineal and curvilineal variations by age, sex, and race.

Perhaps one of the most impressive statistics is the finding that a far larger proportion of blacks of both sexes needed dental care than was true of whites—impressive if it points toward the establishment of "Denticare" for the aged. However, the average simplified oral hygiene index is better for black males, seventy-five to seventy-nine years of age than

TABLE 1
SELECTED STATISTICS FROM THE NATIONAL HEALTH SURVEY, 1960-1962, BY RACE, SEX, AND AGE*

Health Characteristic	Black Males	Black Females	White Males	White Females
Average simplified oral hygiene index				
Total, 18-79 years	2.4—	2.0—	1.7—	1.3—
55-64 years	2.8—	2.7—	1.9—	1.4—
65-74 years	3.3—	2.5—	2.3—	1.6—
75-79 years	2.7—	2.1—	4.6—	1.5—
Mean no. of decayed, missing, and filled teeth,				
including edentulous persons, Total, 18-79 years	12.9	15.7	20.6	21.9
55-64 years	18.4	25.4	21.2	26.2
65-74 years	23.7	26.9	25.2	27.9
Prevalence rates of edentulous persons				
Total, 18-79 years	7.8	17.7	14.3	20.6
55-64 years	19.5	37.0	29.1	39.1
65-74 years	36.3	45.8	60.7	52.8
Average periodontal index, Total, 18-79 years	1.8—	1.4—	1.3—	0.8—
Percent of dentulous adults needing early dental				
care, Total, 18-79 years	65.9	57.5	42.9	32.7
55-64 years	78.5	79.2	46.4	31.3
Mean serum cholesterol levels,* 55-64 years	230	243	234	265
65-74 years	224	266	230	267
Prevalence of rheumatoid arthritis, Rate/100				
Adults, Total, 18-79 years	1.5	4.7	1.7	4.6
Prevalence rates (per 100 adults) for all degrees,				
Osteoarthritis, Total, 18-79 years	39.4	34.5	37.8	37.8
55-64 years	66.3	66.4	63.4	75.9
65-74 years	55.6	75.9	77.5	85.7
75-79 years	78.6	78.0	81.1	90.6
Prevalence of definite heart disease				
% Total, 18-79 years	23.8	24.8	11.5	12.5
% 55-64 years	41.6	52.2	22.5	23.7
% 65-74 years	56.9	70.1	31.3	43.5
% 75-79 years	32.3	69.5	39.3	44.8
Prevalence rates (per 100 adults) of definite				
coronary heart disease, Total, 18-79 years	3.2	2.0	3.8	2.1
55-64 years	5.7	5.5	10.3	4.7
65-74 years	3.4	5.1	12.2	8.2
Prevalence rates of definite hypertensive heart				
disease, % Total, 18-79 years	19.1	22.2	6.5	9.8
% 55-64 years	33.1	46.4	11.7	19.5
% 65-74 years	50.2	66.4	16.3	37.5
% 75-79 years	32.3	69.5	24.0	37.1
Percent reactive to the KRP syphilis test				
Total, 18-79 years	22.9	16.3	2.3	2.1
55-64 years	31.0	35.2	3.5	4.1
65-74 years	32.6	13.1	4.0	2.4
Mean systolic blood pressures in mm. hg.				
Total, 18-79 years	136.2	136.3	130.6	129.4
55-64 years	148.3	155.7	139.7	145.8
65-74 years	158.3	175.2	147.1	159.2
75-79 years	156.5	162.8	154.1	156.5
Mean diastolic blood pressures in mm. hg.				
Total, 18-79 years	83.3	83.2	78.3	77.5
55-64 years	89.3	91.9	82.6	84.2
65-74 years	86.9	89.7	80.5	83.3
75-79 years	84.9	82.9	78.9	79.1

TABLE 1—*continued*

Health Characteristic	Black Males	Black Females	White Males	White Females
Mean blood hematocrit, Ml. percent				
Total, 18-79 years	45.8+	40.8+	46.5+	42.5+
55-64 years	44.2+	42.1+	46.3+	42.1+
65-74 years	44.1+	41.9+	45.9+	43.3+
Mean glucose levels in mg. %				
Total, 18-79 years	118.5	126.1	115.4	126.5
55-64 years	131.7	141.9	130.2	145.5
65-74 years	150.8	166.2	139.0	159.5
75-79 years	201.1	187.2	151.6	177.5
Distance Vision, 20/20 or better Uncorrected				
Acuity, Rate/100 adults, Total, 18-79 years	60.0	52.9	57.3	50.4
55-64 years	23.0	12.9	25.1	17.8
65-74 years	15.3	10.2	8.8	2.4
Near Vision, 14/14 or better, Uncorrected				
Acuity, Rate/100 adults, Total, 18-79 years	47.8	45.6	47.3	26.7
Hearing Level (−5dB or less at 1000 cycles/second)				
Rate/100 population, Total, 18-79 years	62.3	63.2	56.1	60.8
55-64 years	38.8	47.7	44.8	36.1
65-74 years	27.7	32.6	25.1	24.2
75-79 years	30.1	10.2	10.2	8.9
Prevalence of Self-reported Nervous Breakdowns				
% Total, 18-79 years	2.8	10.4	3.2	6.0
% 18-79 years	4.2	24.4	5.6	11.6
% 65-74 years	8.2	23.5	5.2	9.7

− = the higher the score the less desirable; + = the lower, the less desirable.

* All data projected for the United States population, 18-79 years of age, with the specific exception of that for mean serum cholesterol levels, which applies only to the sampled whites and the Southern blacks in the Health Examination Survey.

Source: U. S. Public Health Service, National Center for Health Statistics. "Vital and Health Statistics, Data from the National Health Survey, "Series 11, # 3, 5, 6, 7, 9, 10, 12, 13, 15, 16, 17, 18, 22, 23, 24, 25, 26, 27, 34, 36, and 37.

for white males of corresponding ages. Also *fewer* edentulous persons, sixty-five to seventy-four years of age, were found among the blacks than the whites.

Rheumatoid arthritis was more prevalent among females than among the males of both races. With the exception of black males, osteoarthritis tended to increase with age. For the black males, osteoarthritis was curvilineally related to age.

Definite heart disease was more prevalent among blacks than whites and females than males, with the exception of those seventy-five-seventy-nine years of age. Coronary heart disease was more prevalent among whites, while hypertensive heart disease was more typical of blacks. Curvilineal rates by age characterized coronary and hypertensive heart patterns among the blacks and the latter among white females. Mean serum cholesterol levels were higher for females than for males, whites than for blacks.

The proportion of subjects reactive to the KRP test for syphilis tended to increase with age among all but white females. Mean blood pressure rates were curvilineal with age among blacks and white females. The systolic was lineal and the diastolic, curvilineal among white males. Both black and white males at all age levels had higher mean blood hematocrit levels than was the case for the females, with the latter displaying increases in the later age stages as opposed to decreases among the remaining groups.

Diabetic conditions were more typical among blacks. Mean glucose levels were higher than among the whites for those seventy-five to seventy-nine years of age, with definite lineal increases by age among each group. Black male rates were lower than those of black females until age seventy-five; then the pattern reversed.

In general, a higher proportion of blacks in the late age stages maintained better visual acuity and hearing levels than did whites. The hearing levels of black males, especially those of seventy-five to seventy-nine years of age, tended to be much better than those of their white counterparts. Racial differentiations among the females were not as clear.

Self-reported nervous breakdown data revealed higher proportions among black females than any of the others at all age levels. Special attention should be given to eliciting causal factors contributing to almost 25 percent of black females, fifty-five or more years of age, reporting a nervous breakdown. Some might argue that such self-reported data is unreliable, but it is important to investigate the *meaning* of a situation assigned by the actors involved as well as the so-called objective investigators.

Other data on such variables as chronic conditions, hospitalization, medical visits, and mortality are also available and under systematic investigation. Walker (1970) utilized secondary data in her investigation of relationships between reported chronic ailments and socioeconomic status of the inner-city aged of Nashville, Tennessee. Most of the black and white subjects reported few ailments, but those most often reported revealed certain sex and social class differences. Modal ailments were heart and circulatory disorders among the males, arthritic and other bone disorders among black females, and both skin and arthritic and other bone disorders among white females.

Hypotheses suggested for future investigations are worth noting: (a) the "lower the SES level, the greater the likelihood of a subject feeling ill; (b) there is no significant variation by race for most chronic ailments; (c) where there is such a difference, black females are far more likely to report (or to have) ailments at least partially induced by stress and strain; and therefore (d) both blacks and females are more likely to be affected adversely by the external environment than are white males." (Walker, pp. 50-51).

The higher rates of perceived nervous breakdowns among black females have already been noted, as well as their greater institutionalized rates in state mental institutions in the late age stages. Mental health in old age may be affected in a number of ways. One of the most important issues now being raised in the literature in this respect is the aforementioned one of the impacts of increased black militancy upon the self-images of older blacks. Moore's (1971) failure to realize what is probably the compatibility of Elam (1970) and Solomon's (1970) positions may be due to a tendency to overgeneralize about blacks. Both positions make sense; they must be applied to the subpopulations rather than the total population. A continuing issue about the mental health of the aged is that of their ability to cope with the addition of age discrimination after having already been subjected to racial discrimination throughout their lives. Careful study is also needed here, for data are highly inconclusive (Cf. Jackson, 1967 and Moore, 1971).

Factors affecting the delivery and utilization of health-care services. The work of Fabrega, *et al.* (1969) and Gordon and Rehr (1969) point to some of the problems affecting adequate delivery and utilization of such services. What is most important are their stresses upon the attitudes of care-givers in making distinctions and certain apparent ethnic differences in reaching out for assistance when in need. Probably the most important implication is that black aged, in particular, need increasing awareness of the medical system so as to adapt better to it and make it adapt better to them.

Racial differences in body age, life expectancy, and mortality. The most exciting for me is Morgan's (1968) finding that differential physical aging among black and white males tends to justify assumptions that black males are indeed *old* earlier than white males:

> Negro males of 30 calendar years on have an older body age than their white counterparts. The biggest jump in body age is between 21 and 30, after which Negroes hold a 5-yr. body-age differential until 60 (then increasing further) (p.598).

Such a finding provides further support for differential minimum age-eligibility requirements for recipients of *Old-Age Assistance, Survivors, Disability, and Health Insurance* (OASDHI) so as to reflect racial differentials in life expectancies (Jackson, 1970; 1971c) and, now, body ages.

Additional support is garnered in Demeny and Gingrich's (1967) careful critique of American black-white mortality differentials:

> Unless it is assumed that age patterns of death for United States Negroes were extremely deviant from those found in populations with reliable census and vital statistics, one must conclude that the official figures grossly underestimate early childhood mortality for Negroes, at least for the period, 1910-1940. It follows that, during those decades, *Negro-white mortality differentials in terms of expectation of life at birth were also substantially higher than is suggested by the official estimates* (p. 820, *italics added*).

Finally, Hill (1971) has pointed out that recently the life expectancy for black males has *decreased*. That may be affected by the increases noted in infant mortality among blacks in certain metropolitan areas over the past decade.

Aged sexual behavior. In their mortality and survival comparisons of black eunuchs and intact persons in a mentally retarded population in Kansas, Hamilton and Mestler (1969) suggested that the eunuchs tended to survive longer, but the significant difference found among the comparable whites did not appear among the blacks:

> The difference between eunuchs and intact men with regard to duration of life was significantly more in whites than in non-whites (13.5 vs. 3 years). The detrimental effects of testicular function upon viability, and the benefit from orchiectomy, may prove to be more in white than in non-white males (p. 410).

As in other studies, the small sampling size of the blacks tended to prohibit more elaborate data analyses.

Pfeiffer, Verwoerdt, and Wang (1968; 1969) included blacks in their analyses of aged sexual behavior, most often without racial separation of the data. They held that the "Negro and white Ss did not differ significantly from one another in respect to age-related patterns of sexual interest and activity" (p. 197). If so, their findings are supportive of other accumulating data which refute the notion of "black sexual bestiality." They did indicate the need to study subjects under sixty years of age, and especially women, so as to amass more information on sexual behavior and aging. It would be very interesting to determine whether earlier decreases in sexual behavior tended to occur among black females than white females when they are subjected to more years without a spouse.

PSYCHOLOGY AND RACE

Most psychological literature on the aged has avoided the utilization of black subjects. Where they have been utilized, the problems under investigation have been perceived as unaffected by race. Recent literature has shifted some attention to the dynamics of race and age, with the most significant being that of Kastenbaum (1971), Jenkins (1971), and Brunswick (1969-1970).

Kastenbaum's (1971) investigation of differential attitudes toward future optimism and subjective life expectancies among young blacks and old whites is most intriguing. Noting the foreshortened time perspective typical of deprived, depressed, aged, or dying subjects, he has applied this model to *hard-core unemployed* black males recruited for participation in a job opportunity program (Teahan and Kastenbaum, 1970). Comparisons of those who remained in and who left the program at one and six months intervals led him to the formulation of an hypothesis under further investigation: "there is at least a partial functional equivalence between the phenomenologic world of the young-and-black and the old-and-white." Incidentally, this study also appears promising in the accumulation of more data attesting to the earlier *oldness* occurring among black, than among white males.

Jenkins (1971) has employed an Eriksonian model in providing therapeutic treatment to a young black male experiencing life-adjustment difficulties, and has suggested that racial factors prohibiting adequate achievement of ego integrity in the earlier years are dysfunctionally related to mature adaptation to old age. Thus, he emphasizes the necessity to reform society so as to promote healthier aging among blacks.

Brunswick's (1969-70) analysis of black and white intergenerational differences in outlook on life, interracial tolerance and hostility, and attitudes toward advocacy of violence note especially differential attitudes among younger and older subjects. She has stressed her belief that "education is at least as important a divider, or determiner of generations, as age." (p. 369), and her article is fraught with implications for further investigations of possible generation gaps by age and other variables among blacks and whites. I suspect that self-concept may well be an important divider among blacks.

Byrne's, *et al.* (1969) findings about the relative universality of responding positively to strangers expressing attitudes similar to one's own and negatively to those bearing dissimilar attitudes, portends significant implications for relationships in direct services to the elderly especially, and could, perhaps, be tied in with the Thune (1969) studies of racial attitudes among white and black subjects in a Nashville Senior Citizens Center.

SOCIAL PATTERNS, POLICIES, AND RESOURCES

The bulk of the recent literature falls within the areas of social patterns, policies, and resources. Demographic aspects are also of interest, given the projected data from the U. S. Bureau of the Census (and a possibility that a special report on black aged in the fifty largest cities may be forthcoming from that agency).

In 1970, the reported 1,565,897 blacks, sixty-five or more years of age, represented an increase of about one-third percent over those reported in 1960. As expected, most (56.7%) were females, and most (60.8%) resided in the South. North Dakota had the fewest (twelve males and ten females), while New York had the largest number of females (67,509), and Texas, the largest number of males (50,965). Table 2 contains data on the proportion of blacks sixty-five or more years of age within each state. As shown, West Virginia had both the largest proportion of males and females, while Hawaii and North Dakota had the least.

Hill (1971) has detailed available recent demographic characteristics of the black aged, noting especially their patterns of residence, marital statuses and household compositions,

TABLE 2
PERCENTAGE OF PERSONS 65 OR MORE YEARS OF AGE WITHIN THE TOTAL
BLACK POPULATION, BY SEX AND STATE, 1970

State	Males	Females	State	Males	Females
West Virginia	14.2	13.7	Michigan	5.4	5.9
Arkansas	11.8	12.5	Maryland	5.3	6.0
Oklahoma	9.6	10.8	Illinois	5.2	5.9
Mississippi	9.3	10.1	Oregon	5.2	5.2
Kentucky	9.3	11.1	Wyoming	4.9	6.5
Alabama	8.6	10.3	District of Columbia	4.8	6.2
Tennessee	8.5	9.6	Massachusetts	4.7	6.0
Kansas	7.9	9.6	New Jersey	4.7	5.8
Missouri	7.8	8.7	Rhode Island	4.7	6.7
Louisiana	7.5	8.8	New Mexico	4.7	4.9
Texas	7.5	8.5	New York	4.5	5.8
Pennsylvania	7.1	7.9	California	4.3	5.5
Virginia	6.7	8.2	Idaho	4.2	3.9
Iowa	6.7	7.6	Montana	4.1	5.5
Arizona	6.6	6.6	Maine	4.0	5.9
Ohio	6.4	7.0	Colorado	3.8	5.9
North Carolina	6.3	7.8	Washington	3.7	4.4
Georgia	6.2	8.5	Utah	3.6	6.9
Florida	6.0	6.9	Connecticut	3.5	4.5
Indiana	6.0	6.8	Wisconsin	3.2	3.4
South Carolina	5.7	7.7	South Dakota	3.1	4.0
Delaware	5.7	6.5	Nevada	3.0	3.2
Nebraska	5.6	6.5	New Hampshire	2.5	3.2
Vermont	5.6	6.9	Alaska	1.1	1.4
Minnesota	5.4	6.3	North Dakota	0.8	1.0
			Hawaii	0.8	1.2

Source of raw data: U. S. Bureau of the Census. *Advance Report, United States,* General Population Characteristics, PC(V2)-1, U. S. Department of Commerce, Washington, D.C., February, 1971.

income, education, employment, and health. Of special significance is the fact that he plans to provide a succinct demographic analysis when sufficient data are available. Herman Brotman (Administration on Aging) is also in the process of continuing his highly competent compilation of statistical data on the aged, including black aged, and will be providing information particularly about changes within the last decade. Finally, Inabel Lindsay (Member, Task Force on Problems of the Aging, appointed by President Richard M. Nixon, 10 October 1969) was in the process of summarizing available information on black aged in her role as a temporary consultant to the U. S. Senate Special Committee on Aging (a role which occurred as one of the responses to the *National Caucus on the Black Aged*). All of these compilations will attest to the continued generally low socioeconomic statuses of black aged, and, perhaps, to a slightly rising rate of institutionalization among them.

Utilization of Census and the National Center for Health Statistics data clearly point to the need, as Kent has implied (1971a), for substantially enlarged sample sizes involving blacks, so as to permit far more sophisticated data analyses. Also, given the nature of the times and the need to "check out" the rapidity of change, national data collected at least five-year intervals (instead of decenially) and reported separately (i.e., not as "nonwhite") for blacks would be of great value. The racial separation apparent in the last few years is a welcome step in the right direction.

Familial, kinship, and retirement roles. Major research developments include the likelihood of publication of data from the Philadelphia Aged Services Project under the direction of Donald P. Kent, and from J. Jackson's "Roles and resources of older, urban blacks" (should I cease writing reviews!) within the next year. Such publications will tend to document specific kinship patterns, as well as other data, among urban blacks in Philadelphia, Pennsylvania, and Durham, North Carolina, respectively. As far as I know, no similar studies involving rural aged blacks are underway (in fact, I have not yet located a recent research study on them). These sets of expected publications will probably emphasize strengths and weaknesses of specific subgroups of aged blacks, and the Philadelphia series will provide racial comparisons, and emphasize the feasibility of a network of "caretakers" often found and trained among deprived populations. I wish to again stress my belief that the Philadelphia study can provide an excellent model of "how-to-do-research," for its concerns have not been merely with collecting data, but with providing assistance to the subjects!

My data on kinship patterns and processes among predominantly low-income urban black aged reveal primarily their effective kinship networks or substitutes. They also provide specific information on relationships with parents, children, siblings, grandchildren, cousins, and best friends. The preliminary report on grandparent-grandchild interaction (Jackson, 1971c) shows that the grandparental subjects preferred grandchildren living near them (but not with them) and younger (rather than older) grandchildren. Relationships among their affectional closeness, value consensus, and identification with their grandchildren were unclear, but preferences did appear to be related to particular grandchild types. The data also suggested the implausibility of a general postulation of a "generation gap," because age proved to be a highly insufficient variable, particularly among the males. The findings also debunked the usual myths about disintegrating black families, while sustaining the picture of the important roles many of them actually serve as "Individual Departments of Welfare" when the society fails to provide adequate education, employment, income, and housing for themselves, their children, and their children's children.

"Sex and social class variations in black older parent-adult child relationships" (Jackson, 1971b) did reveal certain significant differences found among a pilot sample of largely middle-class aged blacks in Durham. While most of the parental subjects received some instrumental assistance from children, middle-class parents were more likely than lower-class parents to receive this assistance, and, as expected, daughters tended to be more likely than sons to provide it. The study also suggests the need for greater analysis of parental-child sex preferences in black families.

A most impressive research study in process, particularly by virtue of its utilization of a national sample (3,340 whites and 487 blacks) is that undertaken by Rubenstein (1971). His comparisons of the social participation—largely familial and kinship, among aged whites and blacks has led him to conclude that there are no racial differences in the proportion of those living alone and isolated and in their emotional state of well-being or morale. He does expect to report finally that the blacks fare more poorly as measured by education, occupation, income, and employment, which is, of course, in agreement with existing findings. Lambing's (1969) study of retired blacks in an urban setting in Florida contributes, as well, to a growing body of highly localized data on aged blacks.

Fillenbaum's (1971) report of relationships between job and retirement attitudes found among nonacademic employees in a North Carolina university and medical center indicated that those relationships were quite minimal. She concluded that "only where work holds the central organizing position in a person's life (which here it does not) should job attitudes influence retirement attitudes" (p. 247). What is of greater significance for present purposes is the finding that the white and black subjects could not be racially distinguished by their attitudes toward retirement. However, she did find a racially significant difference in that the negative association between achievement (i.e., "possible acquisition of further knowledge and skills") and retirement typical of the whites was not typical of the blacks. I could not determine whether this was a spurious finding since she provided no *specific* occupational data on the subjects by race. However, almost all, if not all, of the lower echelon "housekeeping" personnel in the populations under study were black, and almost none of the remaining nonacademic employees were in the upper echelon slots at the time that the data were collected. In other words, further investigation of the finding is warranted.

Housing and social resources. A preliminary report from an analysis of impacts of housing relocation among older blacks (Jackson, 1970) revealed many similarities among applicants to an age-segregated public housing complex, as measured by the Carp Housing Schedule (Carp, 1965). The most significant finding is that of the differences separating the successful and nonsuccessful applicants. Briefly, those who were male, younger, and married were more successful, portending grave implications for black aged, for, in some sense, those who were the least deprived were those most likely to gain acceptance by the white admission agents. It would be unfortunate if the usual pattern of rejecting those blacks most in need of educational, employment, and other opportunities comes to characterize the aged as well.

Bourg (1971) has issued a preliminary report on his ongoing investigation of "Life styles and mobility patterns of older persons in Nashville-Davidson County" (Tennessee). This study is primarily concerned with a description of various settings surrounding the elderly and with developmental processes involved in their psychological and sociocultural aging. Findings from his sample of 297 black aged (no other group is under investigation) emphasize their conspicuous diversity "in the functions provided by their social relationships" and their mobility differences. The second phase utilizes a panel of subjects to obtain more detailed information on "the relationship between mobility patterns with small boundaries and dependence on the immediate environment." His study is of special value in that the restriction to blacks only helped to focus upon their differences. He calls attention to the need to explore "the differences amid the similarities" and "the similar components which emerge among the differences."

Lopata's (1970) study of "Social relations of widows in black and white urban communities" could well benefit, from utilizing at least a twofold comparative model: (a) racial comparisons with whites, as she has done; and (b) comparisons holding race constant. Her characterization of the black widows tends to fall within the traditional pathological mold, and one cannot determine readily if the widows themselves were fairly interpreted or if the interpreter unduly influenced her data. Her conceptualization of black widows as being untrained in "skills which facilitate the conversion of strangers into friends" and "often unable to enter any social relation with a great deal of intimacy" (pp. 29-30) represented her value judgement and, perhaps, attests anew to the critical importance of black people performing their own research in such cases. We are given no indication of the variety of black widows located in the Chicago Metropolitan Area.

H. Jackson (1971) has aptly summarized priorities requiring attention to promote the welfare of the aged. The greatest need is for an adequate income, with a minimal floor of $6,000 for an individual and $9,000 per married couple for those sixty-five or more years of age. When necessary, annual adjustments should be made to maintain the equivalent of this income. Other needs given high priority included employment, health, and a nationwide network of community services. In his role as a private citizen and as National Chairman, the *National Caucus on the Black Aged,* he is committed to strive to achieve these goals.

RELATED LITERATURE

In addition to suggested references covering the topics discussed above, the bibliography contains a section on "Additional related literature" pertinent to those areas. They are primarily concerned with the "generation gap," political involvement of the aged, and the provision of social services, such as in health and transportation.

SUMMARY

This third review of social gerontological literature on black aged has focused largely upon recent developments in available data on health and longevity (including body age), psychology and race, and social patterns, policies and resources, as well as related organizational developments. An increasing number of investigators of and investigations on black aged have appeared within the last few years, but none have yet embarked upon a clearly mandated highly sophisticated, interdisciplinary study involving a *large,* random sample of aging and aged blacks throughout the nation. Also, few of these investigators have been black, but the possibility of the development of a social gerontological training program in research at Fisk University may reduce this problem somewhat, as has, indeed, the significant contributions already made by such institutions as Duke University, The University of Michigan, Wayne State University, and the University of Southern California.

There has been far less interest recently in cataloguing the objective social conditions, and far more interest in studying the processes of aging and the specific environmental conditions of black aged. Greater attention has been given to investigations of the influence of race upon aging (e.g., Kastenbaum, 1971; Jenkins, 1971) and upon differences among black aged (e.g., Bourg, 1971; Jackson, 1970; 1971b). More progress has also been made in identifying commonalities among black and white aging and aged persons (e.g., in Kent's Philadelphia Aged Services Project; Fillenbaum, 1971; Pfeiffer, *et al.,* 1969). Two of the most critical research needs are mental illness among the black aged, and trends in the use or non-use of nursing homes by the black aged.

The formation of the National Caucus on the Black Aged in November, 1970, was very significant. It may well serve as a viable catalyst in producing desired research, training, and services for black and other aged Americans.

While it is no longer true that almost nothing is known about black aged, it is still true that we've got a long way to go! It would be helpful if some of the research, training, and service needs already identified here and elsewhere were executed with greater speed. Finally, it would be extremely helpful if Nathan Shock were to extend his bibliographic captions to include a section on "Minority Group Aged."

SELECTED BIBLIOGRAPHY

I. Health, life expectancy and race.

Conley, Ronald W.: "Labor force loss due to disability." *Public Health Reports* 84:291-298, 1969.

Demeny, Paul and Paul Gingrich: "A reconsideration of Negro-white mortality differentials in the United States." *Demography*, 4:820-837, 1967.

Elam, Lloyd C. "Critical factors for mental health in aging black populations." Paper delivered at the Workshop of Ethnicity, Mental Health, and Aging, Los Angeles, 1970.

Fabrega, Horacio, Jr., Richard J. Moore, and John R. Strawn: "Low income medical problem patients: some medical and behavioral features." *Journal of Health and Social Behavior*, 10:334-343, 1969.

Gordon, Barbara and Helen Rehr: "Selectivity biases in delivery of hospital social services." *Social Service Review*, 43:35-41, 1969.

Hamilton, James B. and Gordon E. Mestler: "Mortality and survival: comparison of eunuchs with intact men and women in a mentally retarded population." *Journal of Gerontology*, 24:395-411, 1969.

Metropolitan Life Insurance Company: "Trends in mortality of nonwhites." *Statistical Bulletin*, 51:5-8, 1970.

Morgan, Robert F.: "The adult growth examination: preliminary comparisons of physical aging in adults by sex and race." *Perceptual and motor skills*, 27:595-599, 1968.

Pfeiffer, Eric, Adriann Verwoerdt, and Hsioh-Shan Wang: "The natural history of sexual behavior in a biologically advantaged group of aged individuals." *Journal of Gerontology*, 24:193-198, 1969.

Pfeiffer, Eric, Adriann Verwoerdt, and Hsioh-Shan Wang: "Sexual behavior in aged men and women." *Archives of General Psychiatry*, 19:753-758, 1968.

Solomon, Barbara: "Ethnicity, mental health and the older black aged." Gerontological Center, University of Southern California, Los Angeles, 1970.

U. S. Department of Health, Education, and Welfare, Public Health Service, National Center for Health Statistics: *Vital and health statistics, Data from the National Health Survey.* U. S. Government Printing Office, Washington, D.C.

--,"Binocular visual acuity of adults, United States, 1960-1962," Series 11, Number 3, 1964.

--,"Binocular visual acuity of adults by region and selected demographic characteristics, United States, 1960-1962," Series 11, Number 25, 1967.

--,"Blood glucose levels in adults, United States, 1960-1962," Series 11, Number 18, 1966.

--,"Blood pressure as it relates to physique, blood glucose, and serum cholesterol, United States, 1960-1962," Series 11, Number 34, 1969.

--,"Blood pressure of adults by race and area, United States, 1960-1962," Series 11, Number 5, 1964.

--,"Chronic conditions and limitations of activity and mobility, United States, July, 1965-June, 1967," Series 10, Number 61, 1971.

--,"Coronary heart disease in adults, United States, 1960-1962," Series 11, Number 10, 1965.

--,"Decayed, missing, and filled teeth in adults, United States, 1960-1962," Series 11, Number 23, 1967.

--,"Differentials in health characteristics by color, United States, July, 1965-June, 1967," Series 10, Number 56, 1969.

--,"Family use of health services, United States, July, 1963-June, 1964," Series 10, Number 55, 1969.

--,"Findings on the serologic test for syphilis in adults, United States, 1960-1962," Series 11, Number 9, 1965.

--,"Hearing levels of adults by race, region, and area of residence, United States, 1960-1962," Series 11, Number 26, 1967.

--,"Heart disease in adults, United States, 1960-1962," Series 11, Number 6, 1964.

--,"Hypertension and hypertensive heart disease in adults, United States, 1960-1962," Series 11, Number 13, 1966.

--,"Mean blood hematocrit of adults, United States, 1960-1962," Series 11, Number 24, 1967.

--,"Need for dental care among adults, United States, 1960-1962," Series 11, Number 36, 1970.

--,"Oral hygiene in adults, United States, 1960-1962," Series 11, Number 16, 1966.

--,"Peridontal disease in adults, United States, 1960-1962," Series 11, Number 12, 1965.

--,"Persons hospitalized by number of hospital episodes and days in a year, United States, July, 1965-June, 1966," Series 10, Number 50, 1969.

--,"Persons injured and disability days due to injury, United States, July, 1965-June, 1967," Series 10, Number 58, 1970.

——,"Prevalence of osteoarthritis in adults by age, sex, race, and geographic area, United States, 1960-1962," Series 11, Number 15, 1966.

——,"Prevalence of selected impairments, United States, July, 1963-June, 1965," Series 10, Number 48, 1968.

——,"Rheumatiod arthritis in adults, United States, 1960-1962," Series 11, Number 17, 1966.

——,"Selected dental findings in adults by age, race, and sex, United States, 1960-1962," Series 11, Number 7, 1965.

——,"Serum Cholesterol levels of adults, United States, 1960-1962," Series 11, Number 22, 1967.

——,"Selected symptoms of psychological distress, United States," Series 11, Number 37, 1970.

——,"Total loss of teeth in adults, United States, 1960-1962," Series 11, Number 27, 1967.

——,"Volume of physician visits, United States, July, 1966-June, 1967," Series 10, Number 49, 1968.

Walker, Gloria V.: "The relationship between socioeconomic status and chronic ailments of the aged in Nashville, Tennessee." Unpublished master's thesis, Fisk University, Nashville, Tennessee, 1970.

II. Psychology and race.

Brunswick, Ann F.: "What generation gap? A comparison of some generational differences among blacks and whites." *Social Problems*, 17:358-370, 1969-1970.

Byrne, Donn, William Griffitt, William Hudgins, and Keith Reeves: "Attitude similarity-dissimilarity and attraction: generality beyond the college sophomore." *The Journal of Social Psychology*, 79:155-161, 1969.

Jenkins, Adelbert H.: "Growth crisis in a young black man: its relationship to family and aging." Paper presented at the annual meeting of the Eastern Psychological Association, New York City, 1971.

Kalish, Richard A.: "A gerontological look at ethnicity, human capacities, and individual adjustment." *The Gerontologist*, 11:78-87, 1971.

Kastenbaum, Robert J.: "Time without a future: on the functional equivalence between young-and-black and aged-and-white." Paper presented at the annual meeting of the Eastern Psychological Association, New York City, 1971.

Teahan, John and Kastenbaum, Robert: Subjective Life Expectancy and Future Time Perspective as Predictors of Job Success in the "Hard-Core Unemployed." *Omega*, 1, No. 3, 189-200, 1970.

Thune, Jeanne M.: *Group portrait in black and white.* Senior Citizens, Inc., Nashville, Tennessee, 1969.

III. Social patterns, policies, and resources.

Bourg, Carroll: "The changing environment of older persons," Paper presented at the 35th annual meeting of the Association of Social and Behavioral Scientists, Montgomery, Alabama, 1971.

Cohen, Elias S.: "Welfare policies for the aged poor: a contradiction." Paper delivered at the Symposium on *Triple Jeopardy: The Plight of Aged Minorities in America.* The Institute of Gerontology, The University of Michigan-Wayne State University, Detroit, April, 1971.

Fillenbaum, Gerda G.: "On the relation between attitude to work and attitude to retirement." *Journal of Gerontology*, 26:244-248, 1971.

Havighurst, Robert J.: "Report of a Conference on Flexible Careers." *The Gerontologist*, 11:21-25, 1971.

Hays, David S. and Morris Wisotsky: "The aged offender: a review of the literature and two current studies from the New York State Division of Parole." *Journal of the American Geriatric Society*, 17:1064-1073, 1969.

Hill, Robert: "A profile of the black aged." Paper delivered at the Symposium on *Triple Jeopardy: The Plight of Aged Minorities in America.* The Institute of Gerontology, The University of Michigan-Wayne State University, Detroit, Michigan, April, 1971.

Jackson, Hobart C.: "National goals and priorities in the social welfare of the aging." *The Gerontologist*: 11:

Jackson, Jacquelyne J.: "Social gerontology and the Negro: a review." *The Gerontologist*, 7:168-178, 1967.

Jackson, Jacquelyne J.: "Social impacts of housing relocation upon urban, low-income, black aged." Paper delivered at the annual meeting of the Gerontological Society, Toronto, Canada, 1970.

Jackson, Jacquelyne J.: "Negro aged: toward needed research in social gerontology." *The Gerontologist*, 11:52-57, 1971a.

Jackson, Jacquelyne J.: "Sex and social class variations in black older parent-adult child relationships." *Aging and Human Development, in press,* 1971b.

Jackson, Jacquelyne J.: "Aged blacks: a potpourri in the direction of the reduction of inequities." *Phylon, in press,* 1971c.

Jackson, Jacquelyne J.: "Compensatory care for aged minorities." Paper delivered at the Symposium on *Triple Jeopardy: The Plight of Aged Minorities in America*. The Institute of Gerontology, The University of Michigan-Wayne State University, April, 1971d.

Kent, Donald P.: "The delivery of welfare services: reordering the system." Paper delivered at the Symposium on *Triple Jeopardy: The Plight of Aged Minorities in America*. The Institute of Gerontology, The University of Michigan-Wayne State University, April, 1971b.

Kent, Donald P.: "The elderly in minority groups: variant patterns of aging." *The Gerontologist*, 11:26-29, 1971a.

Kent, Donald P.: "The Negro aged." *The Gerontologist*, 11:48-51, 1971c.

Lambing, Mary L.: "A study of retired older Negroes in an urban setting." Unpublished Ph.D. dissertation, University of Florida, Gainesville, 1969.

Lopata, Helena Z.: "Social and family relations of black and white widows in urban communities." Administration on Aging Publication #25, U. S. Department of Health, Education, and Welfare, 1970.

Moore, Joan W.: "Situational factors affecting minority aging." *The Gerontologist*, 11:88-93, 1971.

Rubenstein, Daniel I.: "An examination of social participation found among a national sample of black and white elderly." *Aging and Human Development*, 2, 1971.

The Gerontologist, 11:26-98, 1971.

IV. Additional related references.

(African aged)

Arth, Malcolm J.: "An interdisciplinary view of the aged in Ibo culture." *Journal of Geriatric Psychiatry*, 2:33-39, 1968.

Arth, Malcolm J.: "Ideals and behavior: a comment on Ibo respect patterns." *The Gerontologist*, 8:242-244, 1968.

Shelton, Austin J.: "Igbo child-raising, eldership and dependence: further notes for gerontologists and others." *The Gerontologist*, 8:236-241, 1968.

(Other references)

Adams, Bert N.: "Isolation, function, and beyond: American kinship in the 1960's." *Journal of Marriage and the Family*, 32:575-597, 1970.

Brody, Stanley J., Harvey Finkle, and Carl Hirsch: "Benefit Alert, a public advocacy program for the aged." Paper presented at the 8th International Congress of Gerontology, Washington, D.C., 1969.

Cantor, Marjorie H.: "Elderly ridership and reduced transit fares: the New York City experience." Administration on Aging Publication #23, U. S. Department of Health, Education, and Welfare.*

Cantor, Marjorie, Karen Rosenthal, and Mary Mayer: "The elderly in the rental market of New York City." Administration on Aging Publication #26, U. S. Department of Health, Education, and Welfare.*

Carey, Jean Wallace: "Senior advisory service for public housing tenants." Paper delivered at the annual meeting of the Gerontological Society, Toronto, Canada, 1970.

Carp, Frances M.: *A future for the aged, Victoria Plaza*. The University of Texas Press, Austin, 1966.

Carp, Frances M.: "Public transit and retired people." Administration on Aging Publication, #32, U. S. Department of Health, Education, and Welfare."*

Hoffman, Adeline (ed.): *The daily needs and interests of older people*. Charles C Thomas, Publisher, Springfield, Illinois, 1970.

McGuire, Marie C.: "The status of housing for the elderly." *The Gerontologist*, 9:10-14, 1969.

Shapiro, Sam, Eve Weinblatt, Charles W. Frank, and Robert V. Sager: "Social factors in the prognosis of men following first myocardial infarction." *Milbank Memorial Fund Quarterly*, 47:56-63, 1969.

Suchman, Edward A. and A. Allen Rothman: "The utilization of dental services." *Milbank Memorial Fund Quarterly*, 47:56-63, 1969.

Trela, James E.: "Age graded secondary association memberships and political involvement in old age." Paper presented at the annual meeting of the Gerontological Society, Toronto, Canada, 1970.

Troll, Lillian E.: "Issues in the Study of Generations." *Aging and Human Development*, 1, 199-218, 1970.

U. S. Bureau of the Census. *Advance report*. General Population Characteristics" PC(V2)-1, U. S. Department of Commerce, Washington, D.C., February, 1971.

U. S. Senate. *Developments in Aging, 1970, A Report of the Special Committee on Aging*, Report No. 92-46, U. S. Government Printing Office, Washington, D. C., 1971.

(References not examined)

Dominick, Joan: "Mental patients in nursing homes: four ethnic influences." *Journal of American Geriatric Society*, 17: 63+, 1969.

Gregory, R. J.: "A survey of residents in five nursing and rest homes in Cumberland County, North Carolina." *Journal of American Geriatric Society*, 18:501-506, 1970.